THEY LIVED ON HUMAN FLESH

is the first detailed, full-length account of the most notorious survival experience of our time: the plane crash and 72-day ordeal of a crack Uruguayan rugby team amidst the ice and snow of the high Andes. It is not one but many stories—

among them:

- the terrifying yet miraculous crash, in which a stroke of sheer luck saved the lives of over half the passengers

- the still-unexplained case of Fernando Parrado, who "died," was buried in the snow—and walked back into camp the next morning

- the agonizing decision of the survivors to stave off death by eating the bodies of their dead comrades

- the racks where meat of human beings hung to thaw

- the incredible journey of two survivors in search of help—a 10-day trek through snow-clogged passes and over 22,000-foot-high mountain peaks

- the nightmare of returning to a world that was mortally shocked by the news of their cannibalism

THEY LIVED ON HUMAN FLESH
is an original POCKET BOOK edition.

They Lived
on Human Flesh

by
Enrique Hank Lopez

PUBLISHED BY POCKET BOOKS NEW YORK

THEY LIVED ON HUMAN FLESH

POCKET BOOK edition published October, 1973

This original POCKET BOOK edition is printed from brand-new plates made from newly set, clear, easy-to-read type. POCKET BOOK editions are published by POCKET BOOKS, a division of Simon & Schuster, Inc., 630 Fifth Avenue, New York, N.Y. 10020. Trademarks registered in the United States and other countries.

ACKNOWLEDGMENTS

I am grateful to so many people who helped in the preparation of this book. I would especially like to single out Dr. Cesar Cecchi, Dr. Eduarto Arriagada, Dr. Fernando Baquedano, Dr. Sergio Valenzuela, Dr. Jose Ansin, Dr. Jose Melej, Dr. Raul Zapata, Claudio Lucero, Corporal Jose Bravo, Ana Astete Percira, the members of the staff of the Santiago Emergency Hospital, the members of the Andean Rescue Corps, officials of the Chilean Air Corps, Pepe, Alice, and Panchi Stevenson, Juan Dustos, who is the editor of *El Mercurio*, and Alvaro Covacevich, the producer of EMELCO films. I could not have written this book without their help.

Millie, Sven, Greg

and Drusie

For Beauty's nothing
but beginning of Terror we're still just able to bear
and why we adore it so is because it serenely
disdains to destroy us.

FIRST ELEGY, 4-7

And we, who have always thought
of happiness climbing, would feel
that emotion that almost startles
when happiness falls.

TENTH ELEGY, 110-113

RAINER MARIA RILKE

CONTENTS

Photographs appear between pages 96 and 97.

MANIFEST

OCTOBER 12, 1972

URUGUAYAN AIR FORCE SPECIAL FLIGHT

AIRCRAFT: Fairchild F-27

DEPARTURE: Montevideo Airport

TIME: 11:00 A.M.

DESTINATION: Santiago de Chile

ESTIMATED ARRIVAL: 2:15 P.M.

AIRCREW:

Pilot: Col. Julio Cesar Ferradaz, Age: 39. Married, no children
Copilot: Lt. Col. Dante Hector Lagurara, 41, married, one child
Navigator: Lt. Saul Martinez, 31, married, no children
Mechanic: Sgt. Carlos Roque Gonzalez, 24, married, one child
Steward: Cpl. Ovidio Joaquin Ramirez, 26, married, one child

PASSENGERS:

The Old Christian Club Rugby Team

Abal, Francisco, Age: 22. Business student. Unmarried
Canessa, Roberto, Age: 21. Medical student. Unmarried
Costemal, Gaston, Age: 24. Law student. Unmarried
Delgado, Alfredo, Age: 25. Law student. Unmarried
Francois, Roberto, Age: 21. Agronomy student.
    Unmarried

Hounie, Alexis, Age: 20. Engineering student. Unmarried

Inciarte, Jose Luis, Age: 23. Agronomy student.
Unmarried

Machirrian, Felipe, Age 22. Business employee.
Unmarried

Mangino, Alvaro, Age: 20. Veterinary student.
Unmarried

Martinez, Julio, Age: 24. Bank employee. Unmarried

Maspons, Daniel, Age: 22. Liberal Arts student.
Unmarried

Nicolich, Gustavo, Age: 20. Veterinary student.
Unmarried

Nogueira, Arturo, Age: 22. Economics student.
Unmarried

Parrado, Fernando, Age: 23. Engineering student.
Unmarried

Perez, Marcelo Ferreira, Age: 25. Business student.
Unmarried

Platero, Enrique, Age: 22. Agronomy student.
Unmarried

Sanchez, Roy Harley, Age: 20. Engineering student.
Unmarried

Storm, Diego, Age: 20. Medical student. Unmarried

Strauch, Eduardo, Age: 23. Government official.
Unmarried

Vicintin, Antonio, Age: 19. Pre-law student. Unmarried

Relatives

Parrado, Eugenia Dolgai de, Age: 43. Mother of
Fernando

Parrado, Susana, Age: 17. Sister of Fernando

Strauch, Adolfo, Age: 21. Agronomist. Brother of
Eduardo.

Friends

Algorta, Pedro, Age: 21. Law student. Unmarried

Etchevarren, Rafael Vasco, Age: 22. Dairy student.
Unmarried

Fernandez, Daniel, Age: 22. Agronomy student.
Unmarried

Magri, Guido, Age: 24. Businessman. Acting coach.
Unmarried

Mariani, Obdulia Yumica de, Age: 22. University student. Unmarried

Menendez, Juan C, Age: 24. Law Student. Unmarried

Methol, Javier, Age: 38. Businessman. Married, four children

Methol, Liliana Navarro de, Age: 33. Wife of Javier Methol.

Nebel, Fernando Vasquez, Age: 23. Bank employee. Unmarried

Nicola, Dr. Francisco, Age: 40. Team doctor. Married, four children

Nicola, Esther Horta de, Age: 36. Wife of Dr. Nicola

Paez, Carlos Miguel, Age: 19. Agronomy student. Unmarried

Sabella, Ramon, Age: 22. Agronomy student. Unmarried

Turcatti, Numa, Age: 25. Law student. Unmarried

Urioste, Daniel, Age: 22. Agronomy student. Unmarried

Valeta, Carlos, Age: 20. Pre-Medical student. Unmarried

Zervino, Gustavo, Age: 19. Veterinary student.
Unmarried.

Flight interrupted at Mendoza, Argentina, due to inclement weather.

Flight resumed at 2:15 P.M., October 13, 1972.

Plane crashed at about 3:31 P.M. in barren Andes Mountains at an altitude of 12,000 feet—a frozen monument to one of the most horrifying ordeals known to man.

AUTHOR'S NOTE

From the moment they were rescued the sixteen young survivors talked willingly, almost compulsively, with numerous people—the rescue team, doctors, nurses and ward attendants at both hospitals; newspaper and television correspondents, relatives, friends and casual acquaintances; waiters, bartenders, bell hops and maids of the Sheraton Hotel; stewardesses and other airline personnel on the plane back to Montevideo; and with home-town friends and casual acquaintances once they got back to Montevideo, discussing all facets of their adventure in considerable detail *before* they ever signed a contract for exclusive rights to one particular publisher. Consequently, without having to contact any of the survivors, the author conducted numerous interviews with many of the above-mentioned people who spoke with the survivors immediately after their rescue.

Moreover, the author (who is completely bilingual) had access to a vast number of newspaper and magazine articles, as well as televised interviews with the survivors. Therefore, he has been able to reconstruct the essence of conversations and personal impressions of the survivors as they experienced their terrifying ordeal.

I

Disaster in the Andes

Arrivals and departures in most Latin-American airports are usually family affairs, with hundreds of parents, brothers, sisters, relatives, and friends jamming the waiting rooms to say *adios* or *bienvenida* to someone they love. There is much joking and light banter, often concealing deeper emotions—tears of happiness and warm embraces for those returning home, tight smiles and held-back tears for those who are leaving. And half-whispered hopes for a safe journey, spoken in hushed voices because most Latins (however fatalistic) have a not-so-secret dread of flying.

Such was the scene at the Montevideo airport on October 12, 1972, where more than two hundred had come to say farewell to forty passengers departing for Santiago de Chile on a nonstop flight aboard an Uruguayan Air Force plane. Among the travelers were twenty members of the well-known Old Christian rugby team, accompanied by relatives and friends who would be cheering for them in a forthcoming match against the national champions of Chile. One of the players was Fernando Parrado, a tall, handsome twenty-three-year-old university student who was a star forward. Unlike most of his teammates, Fernando would have his own special claque in the Uruguayan cheering section: his youngish, attractive mother and a pretty teen-age sister who had always idolized her brother "Nando." His father, the owner of a thriving hardware company in Montevideo, would have liked to join them, but business commitments had forced him to stay home. Nevertheless, Seler Parrado had come to bid his family

19

farewell, huddling with them in one corner of the tightly-packed boarding area where he could quietly urge them to enjoy themselves and not to worry about Dad.

"Take good care of them," he said to Fernando, smiling fondly at his wife and daughter, hugging them with both arms. "I leave them in your charge."

Such perfunctory phrases, repeated so often in so many different places, have become less than cliches, have become almost as automatic and unconscious as clearing one's throat. But each one of those words would eventually come to haunt Fernando Parrado.

Having no premonition of impending tragedy and anxious to get going, Fernando smilingly nodded when his father repeated himself, *"Te las encargo, m'hijo."* Mumbling the customary assurances he casually glanced around the room for a moving-camera view of several other family groups similarly engaged in last-minute embraces and sudden tears. Most of them were well-groomed and stylishly dressed, not flashily or brand-newish, but with the assured good (and expensive) taste one frequently encounters among upper-class South Americans. For this was indeed an affluent group —and politically influential as well. Two of Nando's fellow club members, Eduardo and Adolfo Strauch, were nephews of the President of Uruguay. Consequently, it was no surprise that the Air Force had offered the team and its supporters a free ride to Chile.

They would be riding in a propeller-driven Fairchild F-27, with a turbo engine attached to each wing, the entire upper surface of the plane painted chalk-white except for identifying insignia on the fuselage. The pilot was Col. Julio Cesar Ferradaz, an experienced thirty-nine-year-old veteran who had flown across the high Andes twenty-nine times in various types of aircraft. (He mentioned his cross-Andean flights to one of the more apprehensive passengers who had nervously inquired about the formidable snow-capped cordillera that stretches along the entire length of the southern hemisphere.) His copilot was Lt.-Col. Dante Hector

Lagurara, forty-one, who had recently survived a plane crash without even a bruise. Lt. Saul Martinez was the navigator; Sgt. Carlos Roque Gonzalez was the mechanic; and the steward was Cpl. Ovidio Joaquin Ramirez.

Welcoming the passengers with a firm, resonant voice and reminding them to fasten their seat belts, Colonel Ferradaz maneuvered his craft onto the long runway and almost immediately zoomed into the clear blue sky, both engines humming like monstrous bees as they veered westward. The plane gained altitude as it swept over the lush green farmlands and clustered forests of southern Uruguay to attain cruising level over the early-springtime greening of the Argentine pampa. Nando's sister relaxed her tight grip on her brother's left forearm. The conversation around them was more animated now, boisterous at times. Behind them, close to the tail, someone had started singing a song they had learned at the Colegio Stella Maris, an exclusive Catholic prep school much favored by the upper-middle and upper-upper families of Montevideo. The Old Christian Club, which sponsored the rugby team, was composed of wealthy Stella Maris alumni, most of whom felt much greater loyalty to the school than to the more egalitarian public university they later attended. Recalling those earlier school days, the male passengers were soon immersed in an almost palpable nostalgia, their voices pitched to an *esprit de corps* rarely felt in their separate lives.

"We were like brothers forever bound to each other," one of them later remembered.

As if propelled by their high spirits rather than by their deft hands, a rugby ball bounced back and forth above their heads, occasionally caroming off the overhead rack or dropping into the aisle when one of the women joined the game. Laughter then—and gentle teasing, a *macho*'s grinning affirmation that there *is* a difference, blushingly though wordlessly acknowledged by the senorita who had dropped the ball, perhaps deliberately.

The ball kept bouncing, and the ambience inside the passenger cabin became ever more spirited as the plane continued west on a beeline for Santiago, now approaching a drift of thickening clouds looming above the flat, expansive grazing lands of the gauchos, whose herds of cattle were reduced to mere fly specks on a mottled-green carpet. The clouds seemed to worry most of the women, and they grew more quiet as the F-27 easily accommodated a slight turbulence here and there. Relaying the ball to someone across the aisle, Parrado turned toward his suddenly silent sister and reassured her with a quick smile. "Don't worry, Susana. We're okay."

But when they drew near the eastern slope of the Andean cordillera, less than an hour from their intended destination, the pilot suddenly announced they would be landing at the airport outside Mendoza, Argentina. Weather conditions across the snow-capped mountain range were far worse than had been expected, heavy blizzards having completely blocked all air traffic along the northern route to the Chilean capital. Their spirits considerably dampened by the unforeseen change, the forty passengers tightened their seat belts as their plane slithered through a moderate rain and glided onto a windswept runway now fringed with ever-widening puddles of fresh water.

Glancing at the dark gray sky while the plane taxied toward the airport tower, one of the players predicted a long wait. "Those damned clouds are getting darker."

It was, indeed, a long wait, longer than anyone anticipated—almost twenty-four hours. But during the first few hours the pilot asked his group to stand by, optimistically hoping for a break in the storm on a more southerly route. Meanwhile, some of the men had scampered off the plane to purchase sandwiches and soft drinks inside the main building. Having been informed that candy was scarce in Santiago, they also bought generous supplies of chocolate bars and caramels, numerous bottles of wine, and several pounds of cheese. Back to the plane they went, their arms loaded with packages, their animation renewed. Songs again, jokes about the weather, the women joining in the easy laughter.

Shortly after nightfall, Col. Ferradaz announced they'd be marooned until the following morning, the storms having worsened all along the cordillera. *"Lo que Dios mande,"* said one of the older women, fingering an ebony rosary, "As God wills."

Still singing between nibbles of fruit and cheese, occasionally sipping red wine from plastic glasses, the passengers simply shrugged their shoulders and started another song. Later, when most of them had snuggled into their seats for a long night's rest, the same old tunes were hummed in a low, mesmeric vibrato that sounded like comforting rain.

By daybreak it was still raining. Parrado was wide awake and anxious to take off. He asked the steward about the weather predictions and was told there'd been no significant change; the Andes were still impassable. Later, perhaps. Possibly by noon. Impatient now and feeling slightly claustrophobic, some of the players paced up and down the crowded aisle, now and then peering through the rain-spattered portholes as if to push away the clouds with sheer concentrated eye power.

10:00 A.M.—still no news
11:00 A.M.—increasing impatience
12:00 noon—still no word from the pilot
 1:00 P.M.—the storm may be breaking

Finally, at 1:45 P.M., the Argentine Air Force station at El Plumerillo authorized the pilot to take the southern route over Paso Planchon, the more direct route through Paso de Cristo being still blocked by the stubborn blizzard. He was asked to report his progress to the Argentine authorities as he passed over Mendoza, Chilecito, and Malargue. Once past the frozen hump of the cordillera, he would report to the Chilean Air Force as he flew over Planchon, Curico, and, finally, Santiago.

Pleased to be on the move again, Parrado smiled confidently at his mother and sister as they made the sign of the Cross and silently mouthed a prayer. Singing started up again, with a hint of forced bravado in some voices, as the plane left the ground and grooved through a bank of clouds, shaking slightly in its sharp ascent. Straight ahead were the jagged peaks of the Andes, some of them dwarfed by the much higher summit of a dormant volcano called El Tinguiririca—a tongue-trilling name sounding like an ethereal birdsong. On a clear day, breathtaking vistas would be visible from any angle, and sights beyond all imagining when the mists half-shrouded the hell-deep canyons. But the afternoon of Friday, October 13 was not a particularly auspicious day for sightseeing. Thick clouds clung to the mountains like a heavy gray blanket, and erratic winds bashed against the plane from all directions. Seat belts were tightly fastened even before the pilot gave the alert.

They passed over Chilecito at 2:30 P.M., according to the official log of the Argentine Air Force; then radioed safe passage over Malargue at 3:00. Fifteen minutes later, somewhere above Paso Planchon, the pilot reported to Chilean authorities, noting severe storms and violent turbulence. Then, at 3:29, Col. Ferradaz mistakenly informed the Air Force that he was passing over Curico, a small town in a beautiful valley west of the cordillera and one hundred miles south of Santiago. He had begun his descent through the clouds, apparently thinking he was safely past the mountains.

Within two minutes, strange noises erupted from the plane's transmitter, a muffled desperate order to tighten seat belts. Flying blind, the pilot had switched to instrument control, one of the two engines sputtering as the plane rocked back and forth and suddenly plunged several hundred feet in a violent downdraft, someone hollering, *OLE!* when it struck a second downdraft with another drop of two thousand feet. Hysteria now. Shrill, ear-shattering cries for help; eyes bulging with fear; husky voices suddenly cracking in anguish; someone screaming, *"DIOS MIO! DIOS MIO! DIOS MIO!"*

With the plane dipping and slicing through the cloud cover, the passengers could now see the jagged peaks nearly touching the wings. Seconds later, with a deafening crash, the right wing was torn off, jolting the craft into a narrow canyon where the second wing was shorn away. Then a thunderous, body-wracking shock as the tail was ripped off, instantly creating a devouring vacuum that might have sucked everyone out of the cabin had they been on a horizontal level. But the wingless, tailless plane, still maintaining much of its momentum, now was plunging down the snow-covered slope of another mountain, zooming over the icy snow like a giant toboggan.

Ninety seconds of pandemonium, desperate keening shrieks, and low despairing moans as they slithered toward certain death at two hundred miles an hour—the loosened seats torn from their moorings and crashing toward the cabin; an avalanche of metal, cushions, and trapped bodies, bones suddenly fractured and flesh bruised or torn to shreds. Knowing they would soon be killed—only a miracle could save them—some of the passengers closed their eyes, mumbled half a prayer, and waited for the final crash.

Then, as the plane plowed through deeper layers of snow, it suddenly slowed down—"as if the pilot had applied the most powerful brakes ever invented," someone later recalled. Slower, slower, slower—swooshing onto a more level area where the snow was even deeper—there finally came a shuddering thud as the plane eased into a huge bank of snow at the very edge of a precipice. Had it gone much further—another fifteen or twenty feet—it would have plunged into a deep canyon.

Inside the smashed fuselage there was a dead silence. Then a few moans and mumbled calls for help could be heard. Most of the passengers were unconscious or barely conscious. Eleven of them had been killed or would be dead within an hour. Some may have been frightened to death during that horrifying descent into oblivion. But Roberto Canessa had somehow remained conscious throughout the entire ordeal. He had also survived without a single scratch or bruise. Struggling

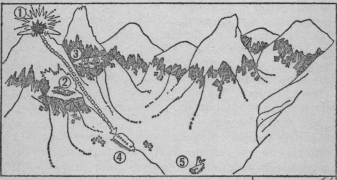

Alto de los Arrieros (1), where the plane crashed into the peak on October 13, 1972, stripping off the wings as the plane plunged down the narrow canyon. (2) Carlos Valeta survived the crash but, in his excitement to reach the other survivors below, disappeared into a snow-covered crevass. (3) The first four passengers died, having been sucked out of the plane, as the tail was torn off. The main part of the fuselage slid down the mountain, stopping at the edge of the precipice (4). Later an avalanche followed the same route, filling the cabin of the plane with snow. The tail of the plane (5) contained the radio used unsuccessfully to call for help.

Camp (6) where three of the survivors spent a night. (7) Route used by rescue party. Tail of plane (8) was finally found three kilometers lower down the mountain. Fuselage (9) housed the survivors during the seventy-two-day ordeal until they were rescued on December 23, 1972.

free of the tangled wreckage piled around him—twisted seat frames, torn cushions, scattered luggage, and limp bodies—he saw that the man sitting next to him was already dead, his left leg partially amputated and smeared with still-gushing blood.

Several other survivors had regained consciousness, and they motioned to one another with tentative gestures, as if they weren't sure they were really alive. In a state of shock, they stared blank-eyed at the terrible chaos on all sides, mumbling the name of this or that friend who now lay dead or seemingly so, crushed in the massive pile-up of detached seats. Gradually, as they absorbed the full meaning of their miraculous escape from death, Canessa and five other men struggled through the debris-strewn aisle, barely hearing the expiring moans and feeble cries of their gravely injured companions, and finally reached the back of the cabin, where the plane's tail section had been ripped off. In the pale light of that cloudy afternoon, they surveyed what was later described as "that awful hell, the sickening mess" inside the shadowed gloom of the gutted fuselage. Behind them—all around them—were the awesome peaks of the cordillera, the elegant cone-shaped El Tinguiririca piercing the clouds at 21,000 feet, more than four miles above sea level. On the slope of the nearest summit they could see a deep groove in the heavy snow, where the plane had tobogganed for nearly a mile at an 80-degree angle, finally leveling off into a huge snowdrift about twelve thousand feet above sea level.

Breathing heavily, for they were unaccustomed to such high altitudes (Uruguay has no mountain ranges), they immediately embarked on the painful task of rescuing those who were still alive and burying the dead. First of all, they removed passengers who showed clear signs of life, handling them with great care and mumbling words of comfort as they laid them in the snow outside the cabin. Then the dead bodies, stiffening in rigor mortis, were dragged through the upward-inclined center passage and deposited in a separate area.

(Taken for dead by someone who didn't realize he was merely in a deep coma, Fernando Parrado was placed among the dead.) The removal of bodies was slow work, made more difficult by chill, numbing winds and increasing darkness, the dull grayish daylight fading early because of the surrounding mountains.

Fatigued almost beyond endurance and realizing it would soon be dark, the men cleared a space in the most interior part of the fuselage, near the pilot's cabin, then brought back inside their still-alive companions, covering them with the few available coats and plastic-cloth linings ripped from the cushions and backrests of several seats. They placed the most severely injured on detached cushions. Now gasping for breath in that oxygen-scarce altitude, their chests burning and their limbs heavy with exhaustion, they partially covered the huge gaping hole at the rear of the fuselage with a jumbled mound of chair frames, cushions, and plastic panels torn from the inside walls of the cabin. "Not enough to block all the winds," they later said, "but enough to keep us from freezing to death."

Meanwhile, Canessa had surveyed the battered, half-submerged nose of the plane. Staring through the broken window on the pilot's side, he saw the bodies of three crew members trapped in a mangle of cracked and twisted metal scaffolds, ripped-apart aluminum wall panels resembling crumpled tinfoil, and shattered glass stained with blood. The pilot was dead, but his copilot, Dante Lagurara, was still alive, anguished cries tearing from his bleeding mouth.

"Take my gun," he implored with tearful eyes. "And please shoot me! Please, please, please—I can't stand this awful pain. I want to die!"

Hoping against hope that he would live, Canessa refused his plea and instead attempted to dislodge him. But Lagurara was inescapably trapped, and there was no way for Canessa to get inside the demolished cabin. Promising to come back, but realistically aware that he must use his waning strength to help those who *could* more surely be saved, he returned to the fuselage to administer first aid to the passengers assembled in the improvised "emergency clinic." A third-year medical student, the only son of a prominent Uruguayan heart surgeon, Canessa would henceforth serve as "director of medical services." (The following day he performed surgery on one of his teammates, using a bottle of after-shave cologne as an antiseptic while removing a broken metal rod from the man's stomach. Though the operation was apparently successful, the friend subsequently died from other causes.)

"Perhaps I should have operated on him that very first night," he later told a Chilean doctor. "But it was already too dark. And I was terribly tired and cold, my fingers nearly frozen stiff."

Fearing the ravages of freezing winds and the danger of an avalanche, the party decided not to sleep that night, although some of them occasionally dozed as the others kept watch. Snuggling close to those less seriously injured so as to benefit from mutual body heat, they talked in muted voices about the likelihood of an early rescue—with, they would later learn, considerably unwarranted optimism.

The search had, indeed, begun. But in the wrong area. At 3:32 P.M., three minutes after the pilot had erroneously announced he was over Curico and starting his descent, the Santiago control tower had tried to establish contact with the F-27, but received no answer. Again and again they tried to communicate, watching their radar for some sign of the missing aircraft. Finally assuming it had crashed in the mountains directly west of Curico or in the broad, heavily wooded valley north of that bustling town, the Chilean Air Force immediately launched a massive search that would last ten days. Forty-seven Chilean planes and four Uruguayan and Argentine planes would fly more than 150 hours, carefully scanning an area many miles from the actual location of the crash.

Unaware of this fatal error, the hopeful survivors crawled out of their refuge at dawn, stamping their feet, rubbing their hands and flexing their arms to relieve the numbness, gazing at the sky for a rescue plane. They saw, instead, a most remarkable sight. ("Miraculous!" Canessa subsequently called it.) Staggering toward them, frozen snow tangled in his hair and clinging to his clothes, Fernando Parrado reached out a hand and collapsed into someone's arms. Unconcious but still alive, half-buried in the snow among the dead, his incredibly strong body somehow resisting the frigid nighttime temperatures for several hours, he had regained consciousness just before dawn. Then he had struggled out of his "grave," his mind still in a fog but his enormous will to live propelling him toward the dark silhouette of the plane. Thrilled to see him alive after assuming he had died the day before, his friends carefully carried him into the "clinic" and covered him with several layers of plastic cloth newly ripped from the seats. He was placed near his mother and sister, both alive but critically injured.

Shortly thereafter, having first attended to the more urgent needs of several other patients, Canessa returned to the pilot's cabin to see what help he could render the man who had asked to be shot, Lt. Col. Lagurara. He was dead—his head tilted back, his eyes staring at the smashed ceiling, his mouth half-open as if pleading once more for a quick death. Looking away, a heavy lump in his throat, Canessa walked slowly back to the rear end of the fuselage.

Besides Lagurara, the eleven others who had died during or immediately after the crash were: Francisco Abal, Fernando Vasquez Nebel, Obdulia Yumica de Mariani, Esther Horta de Nicola, Daniel Urioste, Julio Martinez, Gaston Costemalle, Colonel Farradas, Ovidio Joaquin Ramirez, Saul Martinez, and Carlos Valeta Vallendor.

The death of Carlos Valeta had been the most ironic. When Canessa and his four aides had first emerged from the wrecked plane, about fifteen minutes after the accident, they had seen Valeta scrambling down the icy slope of the mountain. Along with four other passengers seated in the tail section, he apparently had been whisked out of the plane by the powerful vacuum-suction which occurred when the tail was torn off. Having safely tumbled into a cushion of snow and subsequently noting there were other survivors about 3000 feet below him, he had waved his arms like a happy child. Then, as he started down a steep cliff, perhaps too careless in his exuberance, he suddenly disappeared into a snow-covered crevass, never to be seen again.

"That was an awful thing to see," Adolfo Strauch later commented. "He seemed so excited. Then suddenly he was gone. Gone forever. The snows at that altitude never completely melt away, not even in mid-summer."

But on the early-spring morning after the accident (the seasons are reversed below the equator, so that October 14 would be comparable with April 14 in the United States), the sun was hot enough to cause trouble. Melting the surface of the snow so that it glistened after the nightly freeze, the sun's brilliant rays were creating a glare that could eventually cause blindness. Moreover, the sun might possibly melt the bulky snow-drift that served as a barrier against a further downward slippage of the twenty-ton fuselage. It now rested fifteen feet away from the edge of the cliff. "We'd be smashed to pieces if it should slip off this ledge," someone gloomily observed. Knowing the risk, the survivors covered the banked snow with metal frames, sheets of plastic paneling, and anything else that could ward off the sunlight.

Though all the able-bodied men joined in what would be a daily effort to keep the snow from melting away, each one of them automatically assigned himself a special task that was related to his prior training. Roberto Canessa would be in charge of medical services, aided by Gustavo Nicolich, a veterinary student. Jose Luis Inciarte, an agronomy student, would direct a team of university classmates in a search for edible plants. They would also be in charge of rationing the chocolate, cheese and wine which had been purchased in Mendoza.* Two architectural students assumed responsibility for restructuring the fuselage, devising ingenious methods for plugging holes in the makeshift partition across the huge rear gap. They also fabricated "mattresses" with the foam-rubber stuffing inside the seat cushions and backrests. Engineering problems were handled by Roy Harley Sanchez, an engineering student, who would later retrieve a radio from the detached tail section.

Although unconscious or semiconscious during the first two or three days, Fernando Parrado was to become the chief organizer and spiritual leader of the entire group. Had he been able to see and hear the bustling activity all around him in those initial forty-eight hours, he would have felt great pride in his old friends, for those were the most difficult days. While still in a state of shock, and mourning the loss of dear friends and relatives, they had to bury the corpses, take care of the injured, build a shelter against fierce winds and sub-zero temperatures, scrounge for new sources of food, and keep a sharp lookout for rescue planes, working themselves to the very brink of exhaustion in an alien climate and an altitude none of them had ever experienced before. Dizzy and lightheaded from lack of oxygen in that thin air, chests heaving with sharp pains, legs dragging through slippery snow, arms hanging like lead weights, they went about their chores with a desperate determination.

"We had great faith in God," one subsequently said. "And that sustained us—even in the darkest hours."

But some of their confidence must have been shaken after the second afternoon, when they spotted a four-engine jet airliner flying high above them, ten or twelve thousand feet beyond the summit of Tinguiririca. Hurriedly grabbing sheets of aluminum from the remnants

---

* They eventually told reporters that they'd bought 100 pounds of chocolates and 220 pounds of cheese, unlikely quantities for so few passengers. The figures were probably exaggerated for reasons that would soon be apparent.

of the torn left wing, two of the men used them as reflectors to signal for help and to pinpoint their location to the pilot. Seemingly catching the flashing signals, the pilot swerved his aircraft around and executed a giant cross pattern in the cloudless blue sky. "He sees us!" someone yelled, jumping up and down and waving his hands. "We're going to be saved!" That expectation was felt by everyone else. They did not know that at such an altitude it was impossible to spot the white fuselage half buried in the blinding-white snow. Consequently, they were to wait in vain for the follow-up rescue planes, and they would never find out why the jet had made that promising maneuver.

On the following day, October 16, Fernando Parrado finally regained full consciousness, suddenly emerging from his deathly coma like a swimmer bursting to the surface after a steep dive. It was then that he learned his mother was dying, critically injured and much too weak to withstand the warm-to-freezing temperatures. Some thirty or forty hours later, she died in his arms, mumbling the names of her husband, her daughter, and her son. Even though he knew she was dead, Parrado tried to resuscitate her with mouth-to-mouth breathing, tried desperately to transfer his life to her. Numb with grief, he helped carry her body from the cabin to the burial area, where he silently watched his friends scrape a narrow six-foot groove next to several others. Tenderly placing her in this shallow space, he then took a handful of snow and tossed it over her body, closing his eyes in anguished prayer as the others covered the grave with a mound of snow.

Now he was faced with a troubling dilemma. Should he tell his gravely ill sister about their mother's death? Fever-weakened and only semiconscious, Susana may not have been aware of her mother's painful last struggle to stay alive. But surely, in one of her infrequent lucid moments, she would eventually notice that her mother was missing. Nevertheless, Parrado initially decided not to tell her, fearing the news would have a serious effect on her already precarious condition.

Later, however, when Susana kept asking, "Where's my mother?" he realized it would be impossible to avoid telling her. Having first discussed the matter with Roberto Canessa, who promised to stand by in case of a traumatic reaction, he held her in his arms and quietly told her the truth, saying that it was God's will. There were tears and muted grief, but Susana was too weak to muster an emotional outburst, and perhaps too dazed (for lack of oxygen) to feel the harsh impact of death.

Determined, in spite of his personal sorrow, to do his share of work, Parrado immediately busied himself with numerous tasks. Despite his prolonged unconsciousness, he seemed completely alert and surprisingly strong. This was, indeed, an exceptional case, according to Dr. Cesar Cecchi, a brilliant and well-known Chilean doctor. "There are cases of immediate and complete recovery from a deep coma—rare, of course, because such a condition would indicate severe trauma to the brain, a serious concussion, from which recovery is usually quite gradual—a matter of weeks, perhaps several months. But here we have a complicating factor, the scarcity of oxygen, the lack of which can seriously damage the brain. How Parrado managed to stay alive under such circumstances is a mystery. And even though he survived, one would have anticipated severe and permanent brain damage. Certainly, no doctor would expect him to snap out of a three-day coma and immediately function like a healthy man; that's really incredible. He must have a remarkable physical make-up, a unique metabolic system—and a profound will to live."

One should note that "parrado" means "standing up" in Spanish—a most appropriate name.

II

Death in an Avalanche

On the third or fourth day, they saw another plane overhead, a turbo-prop flying much lower than the jet airliner. It practically skimmed the frozen summit of Tinguiririca and then made a return pass almost directly above them.

"It's a rescue plane," someone yelled. "The pilot just gave us a signal—he dipped his wings."

Alfredo Delgado had found an emergency manual in the magazine rack, in which were included various instructions for survivors of air crashes. "First of all," he said, glancing at the first page, "we're supposed to make a huge cross in the snow. Seeing this sign, the pilot will fly a cross pattern to indicate that he's seen the survivors."

"How about the wing signal?" someone interrupted.

"I'm coming to that," said Delgado, a law student, who had already acquired the step-by-step caution of a lawyer. "The manual says that in certain parts of the cordillera, where severe turbulence makes it impossible for a plane to execute a cross pattern, the pilot will dip his wings up and down."

"That's what he did," said Mangino, shading his eyes to watch the retreating plane. "He dipped his wings. We're going to be saved."

"I'm not so sure," said the naturally skeptical Delgado. "Air turbulence may have caused the wings to flap that way."

"But he *had* to see us, Alfredo. This is a pretty big plane—even without the wings and tail. We're easy to see."

"Maybe not," said Parrado, his eyes squinting in the dazzling glare of sun-on-snow. "This fuselage is white on top and half-buried in the snow. It may look like another snowdrift from that altitude. So I guess we ought to make that cross right now—down there, perhaps." He was pointing toward the base of the mountain, at a flat area later identified as a frozen lake.

Immediately accepting the suggestion, four or five men cautiously descended into the valley, using cushions or slats of aluminum for snowshoes. Their eyes closed to slits in order to ward off the blinding whiteness, their bodies crouched against the wind, they thrashed through the heavy snow and created two narrow, knee-high grooves about three hundred feet long, intersecting in the middle. Hours later, as they looked down at their work from a high ledge, one of them proudly said, "That's a beautiful cross—and big enough for even God to see."

"But not for long," Alfredo said with a glance at the darkening sky. "The first big snow will blot it away."

"You're always so cheerful, Alfredo. How do you feed such compulsive optimism?"

"I eat steak every night, my friend. There is nothing better for good cheer."

The mention of steak provoked wry smiles. They had eaten nothing but chocolate and cheese since the accident, and a few nibbles of canned shrimp which Gustavo Nicolich had bought in Mendoza. The first "mess sergeant" was Roy Harley, a twenty-year-old engineering student, whose slide-rule mind enabled him to make very exact calculations in the daily rationing of scarce food supplies. Every chocolate bar was cut into squares measuring so many fractions of an inch. So was the cheese. Using the plastic cap of a deodorant container, he would pour each person an equally exact portion of wine while it lasted—once prompting Carlos Paez to complain jokingly that he'd been shorted seven drops. Tobacco was also initially scarce, causing someone to wonder if Roy had calculated the exact number of drags in every cigarette, assuming, of course, that each person could inhale only six seconds. Fortunately, they later discovered a huge cache of cigarettes in the ripped-off tail section of the plane—130 cartons of assorted brands such as La Paz, Nevada, and Kendall—no doubt intended for the black market in Chile. Since there were only thirteen smokers in the group, each one would have ten cartons. Making a gloomy projection, Roy cautiously assigned each person a half-pack a day.

Though no one expected to be marooned long enough to exhaust the tobacco ration, all soon realized it would be necessary to somehow supplement their dwindling supply of cheese and chocolate. Jose Luis Inciarte, the agriculture student, who had considerable knowledge of flora and fauna, searched all over for anything that might be edible. But, located high above timberline, the area had no trees, plants, or animals of any kind. "Nothing grows at this altitude," he told Parrado. "Except, perhaps, a few tough species of fungus plants that cling to the underside of certain rock formations." Later that afternoon, having dug through huge mounds of snow, he found some lichens that he considered slightly nourishing though not very tasty. They were, in fact, quite acrid and hard to chew.

But a few days later, Inciarte came across an unusual phenomenon: He found some flies and a bee. Astonished and pleased, he scoured the nearby area, digging away vast quantities of snow in a vain search for a beehive. "It would have been amusing to watch Roy measuring one-tenth of a teaspoon of honey for each person." How and why those flies and the bee got to such an altitude remains a mystery. Perhaps they were on the plane when it left Uruguay.

There was no need to be very stingy with the water. Once they had perfected an apparatus for converting snow into drinkable water, there was plenty for everyone. Adolfo Strauch, one of the architecture students, who was soon designated "official inventor," was the man who devised the contraption subsequently tended by Ramon Sabella, henceforth known as "Commisioner

of Water Supplies." Using the detached metal arm of a
seat, Strauch constructed a triangular funnel, one end
flattened out to hold a mound of clean snow, which
would melt in the sun and drip into the downward-
slanted narrower end that was carefully poised over the
open neck of an empty wine bottle. Sabella found his
job somewhat tedious, but occasionally passed the time
guessing the number of drops it would take to fill a
bottle. But it was simpler to guess how many would
drip in ten minutes. (Prisoners of war frequently engage
in similar time-consuming distractions.)

Strauch also produced what some survivors regarded
as his most useful invention: sunglasses. He later told
reporters, "Fortunately, the amber-colored plastic windshield of the pilot's cabin was not completely shattered.
So I took the larger pieces and cut out oval-shaped
'lenses' with a nail file that worked like a glass cutter.
Took an awful lot of patience, but it worked fairly
well. Then I used strips of rubber cord for the frames
and ear loops, which made them look like ski goggles."

"They were great!" added Parrado.

Most of the passengers had intended to buy goggles
at a Chilean ski resort, so only two or three had them
stashed in their luggage. But they had packed plenty of
ski clothes, which they now urgently needed. Shivering
in their light spring jackets, Canessa and three other
men had climbed up the slope in search of suitcases
scattered here and there in the downward rush of the
tobogganing fuselage. Some were immediately found in
perfect shape, others badly battered or smashed open,
and several apparently had been lost in deep drifts.
Consequently, some of the survivors continued searching compulsively for their luggage several weeks after
the crash, as if there were precious objects inside their
valises.

But during the first few days, there was no time for
such idle abstraction. There were too many vital tasks
to look after. As a result, when the ten or twelve most
active survivors had finished their daily chores, they
were glad for a chance to rest. With the sun setting

early behind the high mountain range, at approximately 6:00 P.M., they would creep cautiously into the darkened interior of the fuselage so as not to disturb any patients who might be sleeping. Most of the time, however, their injured companions would be wide awake and anxious to hear the latest news from "the outside world." Had they seen any more rescue planes? Had Jose found any more insects? Would Roy ease the tobacco ration?

Yet no one would ask the most painful question: *Had anyone died that day?* In such close quarters, it was unnecessary to ask. The all too frequent deaths were known instantly by everyone except the patients too ill to be aware of anything beyond their own misery. Some were feverish, or suffering retrograde amnesia that completely erased any memory of the accident. But after a while—through sheer necessity—it became possible to ignore their moans and sudden rantings, and to carry on fairly reasonable conversations.

Snuggling into their improvised sleeping bags, which they had made with the foam-rubber insulation of the plane's refrigeration unit, they would start chatting about anything that came to mind. Some would repeat favorite jokes or tell anecdotes about their family life. Others would describe their immediate reactions during or after the accident. Antonio Vicintín, for example, told how he had escaped death through mere chance.

"I was sitting at the rear of the plane, in the very last row, when we left Montevideo. But after we had got off to buy candy at the airport in Mendoza, I sat next to 'Moncho' Sabella in one of the middle rows, right in the wing section. So I had a fantastically clear view of the right wing when it was ripped off. If I'd stayed in my old seat, I would have been sucked out of the plane when the tail was knocked off. Just like Valeta. So luck was on my side. And yet someone sitting near me was instantly killed—Fernando Vasquez, whose right leg was almost completely amputated when a seat snapped loose. It was so damned weird, this thing of who died and who didn't."

Vicintin would later learn of three even luckier breaks. Gilberto Regules, one of the rugby players, overslept and arrived too late at the Montevideo airport, missing the fatal flight by less than ten minutes. Alfredo Sibils Canbarrere, another player, had decided at the last minute to stay home to study for some exams. And Robert Yaugust, another player, whose father was general manager of KLM Airlines in Montevideo, had decided to take a more comfortable "free ride" on the Dutch carrier. He was already in Santiago when news of his teammates' disaster was broadcast.

Wondering what had happened to Regules in one of their nightly chats (about a week after the accident), someone surmised that he had a flat tire on the way to the airport.

"I don't think so," said Diego Storm, another medical student. "Knowing Gilberto, I'll bet he overslept."

"I can see him now," said Carlos Paez, lighting a cigarette and taking a deep drag. "Sitting at one of the corner tables at Otto's with his girl friend, having his second drink, and waiting for the waiter to bring him Vienna sausage with sauerkraut."

"No, no, Carlitos," someone interrupted. "He would ask for the *Brotola Orly,* the casserole with clams."

"You're wrong, Jose. I'm sure Gilberto would never order that. He hates clams. And, besides, they aren't very good at Otto's."

"You're crazy, man. That's the house specialty! You just don't know good food."

"And I suppose you're the big expert, the big-shot gourmet!"

"Hold it there," said Dr. Nicola, the team physician, sensing the start of a nasty argument. "Let's not argue about who's eating what or where. It makes no difference what Gilberto's eating. Now let's talk about something else."

"How about movies, Doctor?" someone asked.

"Movies are fine. But no more arguments, please."

At forty, Dr. Francisco Nicola, whose wife had died shortly after the accident, was the oldest among the

survivors and therefore considered the *paterfamilias*—
though he could not fulfill that role actively, since he,
too, had been seriously injured and required from
others the care that he, himself, would logically have
been the one to administer. Still, he was a valued
counselor. Realizing squabbles—perhaps violence—
would break out when people lived so close together,
some of them suffering great pain and plagued by the
fear of death, while others ached with fatigue, Dr.
Nicola would try to forestall any serious arguments by
cutting them off at the earliest hint of irritation. But
disputes were inevitable, even among old friends. (He
had undoubtedly read about a much-publicized murder
on an Arctic ice floe, when the crew of a United States
naval ship had been marooned. One of the sailors had
killed a crewmate in a quarrel over a bottle of liquor.)
Also, accounts were numerous of men becoming vi-
olently "stir crazy" in prison or military camps, and
one had to admit that the snow-submerged fuselage and
the surrounding frozen cordillera constituted a prison.
Without walls or bars—but still a prison. He would
mention the danger of men going "stir crazy" to
Roberto Canessa, the group's medical director. Suffering grave injuries, Dr. Nicola had been unable to
help anyone—not even his wife. He could merely offer
advice and hope for an early rescue.

Meanwhile, the conversation had switched from food
to movies, Nicolich giving a detailed rerun of an
Italian movie he had seen at the popular Cine Rex, and
someone else remembered a Sophia Loren film at the
Cine Trocadera. Finally, it would be time to sleep. But
before they called it a night, Sabella would lead them
in the evening prayer that had become a regular ritual,
everyone closing his eyes and praying more fervently
than ever before. Following this, in the shrouded darkness of the cabin, with the shrill night wind piercing
through a crevice that hadn't been covered, someone
started humming a song they'd all learned at the
Colegio Stella Maris.

Sleep, then. But only a fitful sleep. Numb and

trembling in the near-zero temperature inside their "dormitory," they were nestled body-to-body like canned sardines—the more able-bodied volunteering to sleep on the exposed outer flanks, their backs chilled to the bone. Those too injured to endure bodily contact were covered with homemade blankets, pathetically thin patchworks of cloth taken from seat cushions and backrests. Groaning through chattering teeth that gave their moans an eerie, tremulous sound, they could as easily die of pneumonia as from their injuries. Even those who weren't sick faced that danger. Consequently, there was a desperate urgency in their clinging together. But the bodily warmth thus achieved (never more than minimal) had certain drawbacks. Occasionally someone's chapped fingers would rub against the swollen blistered lips of the man next to him, or his bristly beard would scratch the other man's frostbitten ears, and insults would start to fly.

The eighth night was full of anguish for Fernando Parrado. His sister Susana's condition had become critical. Suffering multiple fractures and severe contusions to her face and body, she had struggled valiantly to survive. Both Canessa and Parrado had spent hours near her side, encouraging her to hang on and yet not wanting to prolong her agony. They applied compresses to her pus-infected wounds, touching them with tender care, and periodically soothed her fevered brow with strips of shirt-cloth dipped in water. But all was in vain. The lack of proper medication and food and the ravaging extremities of the weather had finally taken their toll. After a restless night, squirming in pain and moaning with a voice that got weaker and weaker, she finally died in her brother's arms on the morning of October 21.

When the Christian burial ceremony was over, Parrado stood quietly alone by Susana's grave (next to their mother's grave), staring at the brutal grandeur of the cordillera through tear-filled eyes. It was impossible to believe that he would ever again feel such sadness. And what of his father? What must he be feeling—all alone in that beautiful empty house at Punta Gorda, probably believing they were all dead? Grieving for his father as for himself, his throat raw from restrained sobs, he climbed up the slope of the mountain, trudging through knee-high snow and occasionally pausing to stare at the frozen summit of the Tinguiririca. Shimmering in the bright glow of the afternoon sun, the snow was blindingly white against the clear blue sky, the endless stretch of lesser peaks glittering like massive jumbles of rock crystal.

Susana was the nineteenth victim of the crash. Now there were only twenty-six survivors, some of whom were mortally ill. Most of the deceased* were buried in the row of graves not far from the cabin, but the sun had slowly melted away the mounds of snow covering their bodies, suddenly exposing arms and legs, or sometimes a frozen face. As the days grew warmer, it was necessary to rebury corpses under new mounds of hard-packed snow. Otherwise they would begin to putrefy in the hot sun. And the melting snows were a harbinger of something more serious—if less macabre— than slush-covered bodies: the danger of an avalanche. Already huge masses of snow rumbling down the slopes of surrounding peaks had been seen and heard.

But some survivors absolutely refused to let their spirits lag. One of them was Gustavo Nicolich, the twenty-year-old student of veterinary medicine, whose cheerful optimism is evidenced by a letter he wrote to his parents and fiancee on October 21, shortly after Susana's funeral:

Dear folks, Rosina, and kids:
   I am writing you on the eighth day after the air crash. We're in an absolutely beautiful spot, completely surrounded by mountains, with a frozen lake down at the base which should be melting as soon as we get a spring thaw.

---

* Four or five rear-seat passengers had completely disappeared in deep drifts.

We're all quite well, with twenty-six of us still surviving. It's sad to report that Nando Parrado's sister died today, yet our general morale is unbelievably good, and there's great teamwork among us. Roy, Diego, Roberto, Carlos and I are in great physical shape, except that we've got a bit skinny and heavy-bearded. Last Sunday, a couple of planes flew right above us, both of them making a second pass—which, of course, makes us very happy and quite convinced that they'll soon come to rescue us. The only thing that poses a few doubts is that our plane was off its scheduled route, and they might not have seen us.

Nevertheless, our faith in God is incredible—which is probably true in all cases such as this—but I'm sure He's with us all the way.

You may ask how we live, and I may as well admit that our wrecked plane is not perfectly repaired, and for the moment it's not exactly a Grand Hotel, but it will soon be in good shape. We have more than enough water, since we're always producing it. Food? Well, luckily, I still had a can of "Costamar" [sardines], four cans of candy, three of shrimp, some chocolates, and two miniature bottles of bourbon. The food, of course, is far from abundant, but it's enough to live on.

I miss you all so much, and constantly pray to God that, if He should decide to take me into infinity, He should let me see you at least one more day.

Rosina, you can't imagine how much I miss you, nor can I possibly find the words to tell you. Luckily, I had your picture in my billfold, and I kiss it every night before I go to sleep, just as if I were there at your house, kissing you goodnight. All I want now is to marry you—if you'll still have me. But I can't think too much about all that because I'll cry too much, and I've been told to avoid crying because it will dehydrate me. (Incredible, no?)

Monica, Ale, and Raquel [his three younger sisters and brother], you also can't imagine how much I miss you. You're all I have—and that's why I'll do all I can to stay alive, God willing, so that I can see you again.

We're always making jokes about food. Every day, for example, someone selects an imaginary lunch or dinner; and, of course, not even at El Bungalow could you eat so lavishly—no offense to the Camous, of course. But if I had my choice, I would probably choose the food cooked by Blanca [the housekeeper at Rosina's home], and that wonderful fresh milk she serves. It's incredible how much one learns to value such things in a case like this. There's no place like Montevideo, no place like home, and no one like Rosina.

This afternoon, Daniel, Diego, Arturito, Alvaro, and I were discussing the planes we saw the other day, saying how strange it is that no one has come to rescue us. But I guess we're in a very inaccessible spot, which can only be reached by land. And since we've had a few bad days lately, including several small avalanches, they've probably been delayed a bit. This, and our faith in God, is what keeps us hopeful. We pray every night and every morning, and a different person leads the prayers and gives a kind of sermon, his own personal interpretation of the prayers. It's one way of reinforcing our faith and bringing us closer together. Aside from the prayers, each of us tells a joke or a personal anecdote every night, some of which are terribly funny. Like the ones about mothers-in-law or fathers-in-law, which I'll tell you someday. Hope it's real soon.

The most amazing thing is finding a new friend here—"Moncho" Sabella. We sleep close together, holding hands and breathing on each other to create warmth on the coldest nights. Had it not been for him, I think I would have frozen to death on the very first night. We hadn't yet covered the gaping hole at the other end of the fuselage. That's the night when the most people died. I particularly remember Pancho Abal, who probably froze to death after using his blanket to cover Nando's sister, the one who died this morning. Carlitos Paez massaged his body, but there was no way to save Pancho.

Well, I must leave you now, it's getting a bit late, and I've got lots of work to do. A big kiss for all of you, and I'll see you again, if God wills. Should this not be so, all I ask is that you have great courage and not worry about me because I'm sure God will take care of me.

Finally, Rosina, I don't know how to tell you that I love you and adore you, and that I miss you in a way that. . . ."

Ironically, as Gustavo Nicolich was writing his parents and fiancee, optimistically surmising that a rescue team was on its way, his fellow survivors received a contrary report. Someone had found a transistor radio in a small suitcase that probably belonged to one of the crew, and the first thing they heard was that the search had been called off. They were assumed to be dead, and the search for their bodies would be renewed after the spring thaw.

Stunned by the news and initially unable to accept it, they huddled in small groups and tried to bolster each other's spirits with not-very-persuasive assurances that an over-flying plane would eventually see their cross in the snow, or that their parents would persuade Air Force officials to renew the search. But a subsequent newscast dampened their hopes. In a more detailed report, they learned that, according to Chilean legal regulations, such searches were limited to eight days.

"That's it," said Canessa, slowly shaking his head. "There's no sense kidding ourselves."

"We've got to find a way," said Parrado, refusing to

accept impossibilities. "We've got to find a way to let them know we're alive."

"But how, Fernando? The radio transmitter in the pilot's cabin is completely demolished. We've already checked it."

"We'll have to build one. I'll bet Roy could do it."

"I've already tried," said Roy. "But I haven't found any power. I'll need some batteries."

"The batteries are in the tail section," said Carlos Roque, the aircraft mechanic who was the only crew member who had survived. "But where is the tail?"

"We'll find it," said Parrado. "It has to be somewhere in this area."

On the following morning, three men set out on an exhausting expedition that ultimately led them to the missing tail section. Contrary to the original assumption that it had fallen into a drift on the opposite side of the mountain, it had somehow tumbled down the same slope as the fuselage, finally landing in the valley below them but at an angle outside their range of vision. Whooping with joy and self-congratulation, they hurriedly searched through the wreckage and found numerous useful items, among them the batteries and the aforementioned 130 cartons of cigarettes. Unfortunately, the batteries were much too heavy to carry up the mountain. So they had to climb back to their camp, get the radio, and go back down again.

This time they were accompanied by Roy Harley, the engineering student, who spent the next three days trying to rig up a transmitter with the shattered parts of the plane's radio apparatus. On the second afternoon, he managed to get a humming noise that temporarily buoyed their hopes, but he couldn't get his contraption to transmit anything. Finally realizing they lacked proper equipment, they attached the now-expanded radio receiver to the batteries and began listening to the regular morning news broadcasts of Radio Espectador in Montevideo. No Chilean broadcasts could be heard. The first Montevideo broadcast they heard re-emphasized what they already knew: Their hopéd-for saviors had given up the search.

"Well, it could be worse," observed one member of the expedition. "At least now we know what we can't hope for."

"We can also listen to the soccer scores," said another.

Such wry humor would turn to bitterness and gloom in the next few days. "I had never in my life felt so depressed," one of the party later admitted. "Suddenly all hope was gone. Our food supplies were dwindling, and Roy had to announce a cut in the rations. But what did it matter? We were bound to starve anyway. Or freeze to death—the weather suddenly getting colder, the winds meaner than ever."

Heavy snows swept through the cordillera on four consecutive days, forcing them to stay indoors most of the time. Imprisoned in the cramped, smelly confines of the fuselage, shivering and hungry, they inevitably started bickering and complaining—the pessimists pitted against the few optimists in dour speculation about the future, occasionally snarling at each other in spasms of frustration. Saying little but observing much, Fernando Parrado would leave the shelter periodically to check the wind and snow, hoping for good weather to liberate his companions from their constricted cell. Soon. Very soon. Or else they might go "stir crazy."

Finally, after a cold windy night, came the prayed-for change in weather. A couple of warm, sunny days, warm enough to create mini-clouds of vapor from the sun-splashed fuselage roof. Pouring out of their miserable "coop," the survivors felt a euphoric sense of hope as they looked up at the clear, blue skies and the blinding sun. It didn't matter that the grave mounds were getting loose and slushy; they were quickly recovered with fresh new snow and re-covered again when that, too, began to melt in the glaring sunlight.

Hopefully planning new rescue missions to the east and west, convinced their luck had changed, they crawled back to their dormitory at sundown and quietly urged their more severely injured companions to hold on a little longer. "We're going to get out. It won't be long. God is with us."

It must have been an angry God. Or at least a capricious one. An hour and half later (7:30 P.M. on October 29), when most of them were settled into their regular sleeping positions, they heard a sudden rumble in the distance, muted thunder far above them. Then, as the rumble grew louder and louder, like a monstrous tidal wave rushing shoreward on a dark moonless night, everyone snapped to attention—most of them freezing with fright. "AVALANCHE!" someone yelled as five or six men scrambled into the overhead rack just seconds before a huge mass of snow smashed into the cabin, breaking through the rear wall as if it were tissue paper and rolling over the nineteen or twenty persons who had been too paralyzed to move or physically unable to rise from their floor mats. A second wave of snow completely covered them.

"Tito" Strauch later remembered that he felt trapped in a wall of ice. "But since the snow was porous, there was a little breathing space, perhaps enough oxygen for a minute or two. Frantically inhaling, I thought: My God! What shall I do? Then, with a sudden desperate effort, I pushed my hand upward—out of the snow. And as I started moving it back and forth, my lungs now bursting, someone grabbed my hand and started pulling me out." His rescuer was Roy Harley. Digging and yanking with the fury of a demon, he pulled Strauch out of his grave, and then the two of them joined forces to save Jose Inciarte.

Meanwhile, Parrado, Canessa and two other men who had escaped the avalanche were employing an ingenious method of rescuing their buried companions. Crawling across the surface of the snow, which was about five feet deep, they would jab their hands into the thick mass and feel around for the heads of those who might still be alive. And whenever they felt someone underneath, they'd reach for his mouth to check for breathing. Then, cupping a hand over his mouth and spinning it back and forth to create an air-pocket, the rescuer would slowly pull his arm away, pivoting it to create a tunnel through which the surface air might reach the submerged man, giving him a chance to breathe until he could be dug out. (See illustration on page 51.)

Working frantically—and with the split-second efficiency and teamwork of a crew of surgeons or a champion rugby team—the survivors managed to save most of the people who had been buried. Nevertheless, seven died: Gustavo Nicolich, Marcelo Ferreira Perez, Daniel Maspons, Diego Storm, Liliana Navarro de Methol, Enrique Platero, and Carlos Roque Gonzalez. Roque, the mechanic, had been kept alive for several hours with mouth-to-mouth respiration, but he finally expired.

Exhausted and heavy-hearted, the nineteen who were still alive dragged the limp bodies outside and carefully laid them near the now-demolished rear wall. They would bury them tomorrow. They would also clear away the new snow tomorrow. Make a new beginning.

III

To Feed on Human Flesh

The following morning the survivors, still in a daze and numb with fatigue, gave the seven victims of the avalanche a Christian burial. The service was brief and starkly simple, spoken in a listless monotone, as if the participants had been drained of all emotion and were no longer able to express or even feel grief. Then they buried the bodies in a space adjacent to the other graves, moving like weary robots and saying very little to each other.

This illustration demonstrates the rescue technique described on pages 49-50.

Later, after munching a little piece of chocolate and washing it down with cold water, they started wearily removing the snow from their cabin. Using broken sheets of aluminum (or their bare hands) for shovels, they worked like stoop-laborers, their backs aching almost beyond endurance, their chests heaving as they gasped for oxygen. They succumbed that night to a sleep as profound as death itself.

Two days later, when the snow had been cleared from the fuselage and the rear wall reassembled, the survivors had recovered their spirits enough to celebrate Carlos Paez's nineteenth birthday. Opening one of the few remaining bottles of cherry wine and diluting it with water, they drank a toast to him and sang "Happy Birthday." And, resuming one of their favorite pastimes, Carlos selected an imaginary birthday dinner from an imaginary menu.

"First of all, we'll have a *pate de maison*—like they have at Del Aguila," Carlos said.

"It's better at the Oscarbar," someone interjected. "Less mushy."

"Shut up!" said another. "This is Carlos' birthday. He can order anything he wants."

"Then we'll have the specialty of the house at Morini's, some *fondue au fromage,* with the cheese sizzling hot . . . or maybe the Oscarbar's *pollo deshuesado a la almendra.*"

"That's perfect," said Delgado, as if the meal actually had been served. "You're a born gourmet, Carlitos. Now, what shall we have for dessert?"

Listening to his friends' approving comments and watching them lick their lips at each stage of the imaginary meal, Fernando Parrado must have wondered whether such a game was helpful or harmful. But even if it *were* psychologically harmful, it couldn't be stopped, for this particular game had become compulsive. Food was the principal topic of conversation, fast becoming an obsession. The group seldom talked about sex—even now, when there were no longer any women to inhibit conversation. Obdulia Mariani was instantly killed in the crash; Eugenia Parrado died three days later; Esther Nicola succumbed to severe internal injuries soon thereafter; Susana Parrado died on October 21; and Liliana Methol, also gravely injured, had nevertheless survived until October 29, when she was buried in the avalanche.

Food, by now, had become the all-consuming passion, the passion intensifying as the supplies dwindled day by day and as Roy kept reducing the rations to fractions of a fraction. "This slice of cheese is so thin I can actually see through it," complained Mangino one afternoon.

Yet they managed to hang on, drinking more and more water to fill their empty stomachs and imagining even more elaborate dinners than the one Carlos had ordered for his birthday. But since their bodies could not feed on fancy alone, they experienced more frequent and more prolonged dizzy spells resulting from a combination of hunger and the scarcity of oxygen. Their stomachs cramped with gnawing pains, their unwashed bodies itching with grime and sweat, their eyes reddened for lack of sleep as they lay waiting for the next avalanche, most of them teetered on the edge of hysteria. Becoming more irritable each day, ready to argue at the slightest provocation, they were advised by Parrado and Canessa to avoid contact as much as possible, to walk away from impending arguments. And to pray for patience. Indeed, the evening prayers and reciting of the rosary had become more earnest, more urgent than ever before—a desperate reaching out for a God that seemed to have deserted them.

"But we would not, *we could not* lose our faith," they later insisted.

Mumbling prayer after prayer far into the night, ears alert for the slightest sound from the outside, they slept fitfully or not at all. One more avalanche would be too much to bear. Even those who managed to sleep would jerk to attention in the middle of the night, caught in a dream of huge masses rumbling down the mountain and completely demolishing their cabin. Or they might snap out of an equally hideous nightmare yelling the name of someone who had died in the plane crash.

Prayers again in the morning.

Then two or three men would climb down the slippery slope to hear the morning news broadcast from Montevideo, always hoping the announcer would mention something about a new rescue mission. Their companions, having very little to do, would sit in clusters outside the plane repeating and re-repeating personal anecdotes with no more interest than someone reading a column of names from a phone directory. Once in a while, someone would take off in search of his still-missing suitcase, pushing and scrounging through heaps of snow like a dog nosing around for last year's buried bone. Such compulsive acts had become endemic, and most of them were somehow related to hunger.

Dr. Francisco Nicola, the team physician, who had worried about malnutrition and eventual starvation from the very beginning, had detected clear symptoms in most of the survivors after the first week. Therefore, just before he died from injuries sustained in the crash, he engineered a long discussion with Parrado and Canessa, sensing they were the natural leaders of the group.

"I know I'm dying," he said, "and there is no way to save me. But before I die, I want to suggest—in fact, very strongly urge—that you do something that may shock you, but which is absolutely necessary."

"We're listening," they said.

"Well, I know this will be very difficult for all of you—possibly repugnant—but I'm afraid you'll have to consume the flesh of those who have already died. Otherwise, you will surely starve to death."

Stunned into silence, awed by the vast implications of what the doctor was saying, Parrado and Canessa momentarily glanced at each other as Nicola continued in a soft, whispery voice:

"Now, Roberto is fully aware of the absolute need for proteins, because he's a medical student. But, Fernando, I want you particularly to realize that a man cannot live without proteins; and the only source of proteins in this area is lying out there in those graves. . . ." He paused, as if searching for an easier way to put it, but knew there was no way to avoid the harsh truth. "I know it's a horrible thought, my friends, but I'm sure those who have died would willingly sacrifice themselves so that some of you may live. There are, after all, other people for whom you should live—brothers, sisters, parents, and perhaps a fiancee. If I were not already doomed, I would do everything possible to go on living—even though my wife has died—for I have four children at home. So I plead with you to convince all the others that they must try to save themselves."

"That's certainly true about the proteins," said Canessa. "I guess every medical student knows that, but I haven't wanted to think about—"

"Well, now that I've mentioned the most difficult part, I would also suggest that you consume your own urine—that you mix it with water and—"

"But, why?" asked Parrado.

"Here again, I guess Roberto will understand more easily. Anyway, Fernando, I want you to understand that urine also contains certain elements the body needs, certain salts and minerals that are lacking in the snow water we're drinking because it's really like distilled water. The salts I'm referring to—which Roberto knows about—are sodium chloride, phosphoric acid, sulfuric acid, uric acids, and plain organic salts. And you must bear in mind that urine also contains proteins."*

Shortly thereafter, he died.

Gradually repressing their initial shock and revulsion, Canessa and Parrado finally had to accept the logic of Dr. Nicola's deathbed advice—but how could they possibly convince the others? They pondered the question during the next few days, unhappily aware that the

* Urea, the chief nitrogen constituent of urine, is a product of the decomposition of proteins.

hunger problem was fast approaching a critical stage. Then, one afternoon less than a week after the avalanche, they assembled all their companions for "a discussion of a most important matter." Their very manner suggested something beyond the ordinary. And because it was essentially a medical problem, it was Canessa who spoke first.

Choosing his words carefully, he told them about the conversation they'd had with Dr. Nicola, repeating his words almost verbatim, for they had been deeply engraved on his mind—perhaps never never to be forgotten. There were gasps of horror from some of the men.

"But that's cannibalism," someone said in an anguished voice. "How could we possibly do such a thing?"

"No, it isn't!" someone else protested. "We wouldn't be killing anyone, the way real cannibals do. These people are already dead. So there's a big difference."

"But they're our friends—some of them our own flesh and blood, Roberto."

"We could make exceptions," said another. "We could agree not to touch the body of any sister, brother, wife, husband, or parent of anyone among us."

Having presented Dr. Nicola's proposal as cogently as possible, Canessa steered clear of the ensuing discussion, knowing that ultimately it would have to be accepted or rejected on another plane—with the scientific justification merely buttressing a moral decision to go ahead, or else being rejected outright as morally irrelevant. Thus, it was probably wiser to let everyone pour out his own feelings, pro or con, to wrestle with his own soul without undue pressure from anyone else. Yet, as Dr. Nicola had noted in his parting words, "It will be easier if you can get everyone to accept this decision. Any dissenters—even one—would make the others feel guilty. So it's almost necessary to reach a common accord."

Easier said than done. Too much insistence could trigger completely negative reactions, particularly when dealing with a taboo so universally accepted, so deeply ingrained in the human psyche. So Parrado, Canessa, and a growing list of allies would have to persuade the others with "great tact and gentle concern," uneasily conscious that time was running against them, that the symptoms of incipient starvation were already present.

Perhaps it was excruciating hunger itself that finally persuaded the most stubborn dissenters to accept Dr. Nicola's advice. But some of them (Roy Harley, Numa Turcatti, and two or three others) were never fully convinced. They went along with the consensus because they were essentially team players. Nevertheless, two of the younger men later became quite hysterical and threatened to commit suicide or simply let themselves starve to death. Realizing this was a serious threat, Parrado hid all the cartridges he had taken from two guns he had earlier found in the pilot's cabin. He and Canessa also had long talks with their younger teammates and apparently managed to calm them down. At least temporarily.

Meanwhile, Canessa with one of his medical crew had begun the surgical dismemberment of the first corpse, which had been disinterred and placed in the sun to defrost. Commencing with the lower extremity of the right leg, using a razor blade, he cut the connecting tendons of the outer *soleus* muscles of the calf and then the more interior *tibialis* muscles, carefully removing the lean flesh and setting it aside. Then he removed the much thicker thigh muscles—the *vastus lateralis, biceps femoris* and *gluteus maximus.* And after repeating the same procedure on the left leg, Canessa and his helper suspended the long strips of flesh from the rafters of the fuselage. "We want the oils to drain into the pans on the floor," he explained to a few puzzled bystanders, most of the others having decided to take a stroll. "These oils will be useful as salves and healing agents."

The torso was defrosted the next day, and the muscles of the stomach were removed—the *transversus abdominus, rectus abdominus,* and *pyramidalis*—after which came the posterior muscles—the *psoas major* and *quadratus lumborum*. These, too, were suspended from the rafters. Then came the chest muscles *(trapezius* and *pectoralis major),* and finally the slimmer arm muscles *(biceps brachii* and *brachio radialis).* The brain, liver, and kidneys were removed later.

The leg muscles having drained sufficiently, Canessa cut them into slender strips, which were then chopped into very small pieces. These, in turn, were rolled into small pellets that could be swallowed without too much difficulty—swallowed raw, because there was no fuel for cooking, the plane's fuel having spilled all over the mountain in its wild tobogganing descent. During the first few days, the pellets of flesh were rolled in melted chocolate and then allowed to freeze before being eaten, but the chocolate was soon exhausted.

Initially, some of the group were nauseated when they saw the hunks of raw human flesh dangling from the ceiling of their dormitory, the oils and blood dripping into makeshift pans.

"Isn't there some other way—some other place— to do this?" someone asked, recoiling from the grisly sight. "This looks like a slaughterhouse."

"Worse than that," added someone else, ducking his head and sidling past the *gluteus maximus.* "And it's beginning to smell."

"It's been smelling pretty bad for at least two weeks," Sabella reminded him. "There've been a lot of unwashed bodies and several very sick people cooped up in here."

"But this smell is different."

"You'll get used to it," said Canessa, remembering his own squeamish reactions when he first witnessed the dissection of a cadaver at medical school. "And part of that smell is in your imagination, Carlitos."

Although many of them would never get used to the flesh swinging from the rafters, or the smell, they realized it was necessary. And perhaps that macabre spectacle made it somewhat easier for them to consume the innocuous-looking meat pellets, especially when coated with chocolate. Regardless of their feelings, which of course varied in scope and intensity, one thing was clearly evident: *Their health immediately improved.* The intake of protein increased their strength and energy, and also reduced much of the dizziness and light-headedness that had plagued them.

One man, however, did not improve—Numa Turcatti, who got thinner and weaker as the days went by, his eyes more pale and watery. Puzzled by Turcatti's failure to respond to the improved diet, Canessa and Parrado began to watch over him with special care, increasing his ration of meat and giving him their last remaining shares of cheese. It was then that Canessa discovered that Turcatti had not eaten any of the pellets, that he had been burying them in the snow.

Fearing he would soon die of starvation, several of the survivors implored him to eat his rations. "Just swallow them, Numa," one of them said. "You don't have to chew them—no one chews them. Just swallow the damned things and pretend they're vitamin capsules. But take them!"

But Turcatti would not be persuaded. Nothing could budge him. "I can't!" he would say, turning away from them. "I just can't."

A few of his closest friends tried to force him to eat, but he still refused. He would spit out the capsules and clamp his mouth tight, his eyes pleading with them to leave him alone.

Finally, after several days of semiconsciousness and occasional spells of delirium, Turcatti died, his once-strong athlete's body emaciated beyond recognition. Once again the death-weary survivors gathered round a mound of snow for a Christian funeral service, many of them inwardly thinking that perhaps Turcatti had been more faithful to his creed than anyone else—that he had also been more courageous. Who would know? Who could finally judge?

Turcatti's death had considerable impact on almost everyone. For several days, nearly a week in some instances, some of the others had difficulty swallowing the pellets. A few kept vomiting or suffered severe cramps and dizzy spells. But eventually they managed to overcome the trauma and once again showed signs of improved health as the much-needed protein seeped into their systems.

Deliberately avoiding any discussion of what someone ironically called "our unique diet," the group resumed their former activities. Several exploratory expeditions were launched, with teams of two or three men setting off in different directions, hoping to find a way out of the maze of frozen mountains surrounding them. They knew that Chile lay to the west and Argentina to the east, but they also sent missions north and south in search of the trans-Andean highway or the railroad that runs parallel to it. They were fearful, however, of wandering too far from home base. For although the days were a bit warmer, the nights were still bitterly cold and the winds savage. Moreover, there was always the danger of an avalanche, which would be especially hazardous in the narrow canyons that were otherwise the most convenient passageways.

In one of their first "blind probes into nowhere," Parrado and two other men were stranded for thirty hours on a narrow ledge of a tortuously jagged peak several miles north of camp. Attempting to skirt a huge protruding boulder just beyond the high ledge, they were beaten back by howling winds and blinding snow blowing off the slope above them. So they retreated to the less-exposed niche they had just left and huddled close together for warmth, unhappily noting that the sky had suddenly darkened.

"We'll wait for the wind to die down," said Parrado. "Then we'll go down the other side."

"I don't think it will die down, Fernando. And I'm afraid it's going to snow. Look at those goddamned clouds."

A half hour later it began to snow, the winds screaming like the *lloronas* or demented witches they'd heard about as children. The new storm was severe enough to imprison them on the ledge all that night, the fol-

lowing day, and the next night as well. Chilled to the
bone and exhausted by a long day of hard climbing,
they spent the first night clustered together, massaging
each other's arms and legs and squirming bodies against
each other to create more friction.

"This would be a lot more fun if you were a woman," someone whispered through chattering teeth. "But
you'd have to be a lot fatter. You're awfully bony
around the hips."

Sometime during the first night, while Parrado was
taking his turn as the stay-awake guard, the storm
faded to steady snowfall. But new, more violent winds
started blowing just after dawn, forcing the party to
remain on the snow-covered ledge throughout the next
day. Fortunately, they had brought along extra meat
pellets, which supplied enough energy for them to
exercise their limbs to ward off stiffness. At midafternoon they decided to go back down the mountain, but
the route they had previously taken (perilous enough
under better conditions) was now too slippery and
obstructed by new drifts.

"We'll have to stay another night," said Parrado,
brushing a few white flakes from his wind-chapped
face. "It ought to be easier now that we're used to it."

Though it was far from easy, they managed to survive another night and arrived back at camp toward
noon of the following day, extremely tired and hungry
—"and awfully damned glad to be alive."

During the next few days, the men spent hours and
hours remaking the huge cross in the snow that was
supposed to be a signal for help to planes flying overhead, thrashing through deep drifts that covered the
frozen lake at the base of the mountain. Most of the
time, however, the cross would disappear under new
snows or would be obliterated by the wind. But as the
snows lessened and the sun grew hotter during the long
month of November (mid-spring south of the equator),
the mounds of snow covering the graves would begin
to melt into slush, and they would have to be replaced
with larger quantities of less mushy snow.

And, of course, the occasional thaws would reawaken fears of more avalanches, nightmare visions of gigantic masses rumbling down the slopes while everyone was sleeping—or trying to sleep. The prayers would be longer then, more intense, more frantic. But there was never despair. Nor self-pity. "And we knew," so they later said, "knew in the deepest recesses of our souls that we would finally survive. That we would not be abandoned. That God was with us."

IV

Desperate Parents
and Clairvoyants

While the stranded survivors suffered the hardships of what someone later described as "the highest hell on earth," their parents and relatives were experiencing a different kind of torment. Some of the more fatalistic "realists" reluctantly assumed that all passengers had been instantly killed or had subsequently died in the vast frozen vaults of the cordillera, especially after the Chilean Air Force ended its search for the missing plane. But a few parents stubbornly refused to give up hope and persisted in believing their sons were still alive.

The most insistent optimist—certainly the most voluble—was a man named Carlos Paez, whose son bore the same name. A somewhat Bohemian artist and writer with a flair for publicity, Paez became the unofficial spokesman for all the other parents and relatives. Casually attired in denim trousers, open-necked shirt and rugged work shoes, he took the first plane to Santiago when he heard the newscast about the missing Uruguayan plane, and he remained in Chile for the next ten weeks, organizing search trips and cajoling the local press into writing editorials and articles demanding a renewal of rescue efforts by the Air Force.

"My boys are still alive!" he would insist, casually assuming the role of father of the entire group. "I know they are still living, and we've got to reach them."

Having accumulated a number of colorful good-luck amulets which dangled from his neck, the handsome, forty-year-old painter-writer became a familiar sight in the editorial offices of newspapers and magazines in Santiago, spicing his pleas for help with off-hand allusions to his own personal background. Thus, between solemn speculations about the possible whereabouts of his son and fellow victims, he told reporters that he had lived at Albert Schweitzer's leprosarium, that he had also lived with the Papua savages of New Guinea, that he was an intimate friend of Brigitte Bardot, that he had helped Jorge Luis Borges write *Mediomundo,* and that he had written various books on his travels through Brasilia, Candombe, and Bahia.

Having been impressed by the voodoo magic of certain Brazilian black people, Paez now sought comfort in the "magic legends" of the ancient Mapucho tribes of Chile, finding in them "certain omens that prove my son and his friends are still alive."

But Paez did not rely on magic alone. Within a few days after the accident he went to the National Library and read every book he could find on the mountain ranges of Chile, absorbing information on weather conditions, animal life at various altitudes, availability of edible plants, and reports of earlier accidents in the cordillera. Among the many books and magazine articles, he found one written by Joaquin Gandarillas, apparently the country's foremost expert on the region surrounding the dead volcano El Tinguiririca. Once again relying on great charm and tenacity, Paez persuaded Gandarillas to accompany him to the western slope of the range dominated by the immense volcano. Obtaining a horse at a small military encampment named Puerto Negro, he rode through the lower valleys and canyons in search of clues. "I kept whistling and hollering at the top of my voice," he told one reporter, "hoping the echoes would reach my son. But he was too far away."

Temporarily disappointed but not disheartened, he returned to Santiago to organize further expeditions, composed of Chilean sympathizers who had read about him or seen him on local television talk shows. By now he had accumulated several additions to the cluster of amulets hanging down his chest—a small talisman made from the hair of an elephant's tail, a dollar "worn backward as a protest against American commercialism," an Indian keepsake, a silver cross, a polished lion's fang, the left paw of a wildcat. "I'm a very superstitious man," he admitted quite candidly. "I close all closet doors at night and never leave an unmade bed when I go out."

Apparently, Carlos Paez's wife was equally influenced by occult phenomena. She and several other mothers met several weeks after the accident and thereafter jointly financed a series of consultations with a famous Dutch clairvoyant, Gerard Croisset. "He's one of the greatest seers in the world," she told her friends in suburban Montevideo. "He's a frequent consultant to Queen Juliana of Holland and many other political leaders who want to look into the future or to find out the secrets of their enemies. So I'm sure he can tell us where the plane has crashed—and if our sons are alive."

More famous in Europe and Latin America than his countryman and fellow clairvoyant, Peter Hurkos (who advises numerous Hollywood movie stars), Croisset was the subject of a best-seller titled *The Miracle Eyes,* which relates several "astonishing feats of extra-sensory perception." His very ardent fans also refer to a theoretically scientific treatise by Dr. Willen H. Tenhaeff, director of the Institute of Parapsychology at the University of Utrecht, who considers Croisset "an exceptionally gifted man, with rare psychic powers and aptitudes." But to most skeptics, Croisset and all other clairvoyants are at best "lucky guessers"—and at worst "expensive frauds."

Expense was no deterrent to the wealthy parents of the missing rugby players and their companions. "I'll pay anything to find my son," one of them asserted at a press conference announcing that Croisset had been retained. But because of prior commitments requiring his presence in Amsterdam, the consultations had to be conducted by telephone and short-wave radio. An amateur ham-radio operator was continuously in touch with Pancho Ibanez, a fellow Uruguayan who fortuitously lived in Holland. Ibanez questioned Croisset in Amsterdam and relayed the taped recordings of their meetings back to South America:

IBANEZ: Where is the missing plane?

CROISSET: Well, first of all, let me give you my impression of the problems that plagued the airplane. Before boarding the plane, I see among the passengers a very fat man who likes Havana cigars but never finishes them.

I see a long table in a restaurant. There are seven people on one side . . . seven on the other. The restaurant has very wide windows. . . . The fat man is not at the head of the table. There is someone else there—a gray-haired man. But the fat man is sitting near this man, who is—well, let's say he's the chief.

Then he and the fat man leave the dining room. . . . I'm talking a lot about the fat man because he has some connection with the pilot.

IBANEZ: Was this the second time they took off?* Or are you referring to an airport that could be in Uruguay?

CROISSET: I don't know, I don't know. I guess it could be Uruguay. Anyway, it was there that the fat man ate something that would later make him ill. Or perhaps it was the cigar. I don't know. But I think it—yes, I'm now sure it was the last meal.

---

* This would be at Mendoza, Argentina.

The plane took off. Now I'm going to draw you a small circle on the map indicating the spot where the fat man began to feel awfully sick. It was before they passed Planchon. You will ask me what made him feel sick, and I'd say it was something he ate. He was also quite nervous. I don't know exactly what bothered him, but he was extremely ill.

IBANEZ: This fat man you mention wasn't one of the players—one of the young players—was he?

CROISSET: No. Perhaps the manager. He was about fifty-six years old.

IBANEZ: Is the fat man tall?

CROISSET: Yes. He has an enormous body. He might have been a rugby player a long time ago. Now he's too old and fat. Also too nervous. Well, that's enough about the fat man. Let's look at the pilot. Passing Planchon, all went well. Then the plane went like this. (Croisset draws a light zigzagging line on the map, which generally follows the original direction past Planchon). The pilot looks to the right, trying to find the route that will take him north. There has to be a huge mountain around here, to the right of the plane. Shortly thereafter the right engine starts making an intermittent rat-tat-tat noise. Something's wrong with the carburetor. I'll explain it to you with a sketch. (He makes a simple outline of a carburetor and points to the fuel line.) This tube was dirty, obstructed, so that the fuel couldn't get to the carburetor.

The right engine started—well, it started missing and finally stopped. The left one was functioning okay. The pilot wanted to bear to the north, passing the mountain on his right, but that's when he noticed his engine was falling. He didn't use his radio at that moment because all his attention was concentrated on the emergency. Moreover, his copilot, who should have been seated next to him, wasn't there. He had gone back to the passenger cabin. Why was he there? I don't know. Perhaps because of the fat man getting sick.

The pilot looks at the wing. Sees that the right engine has gone dead. . . .

IBANEZ: Can you see the right engine from the pilot's seat on the left side of the cockpit?

CROISSET: No, he would have to lean way out, but he didn't have to—because he could "see" it on his instruments, his dashboard. A light goes on that tells him the engine has stopped. So he disconnects the radio. . . .

IBANEZ: The radio?

CROISSET: I'm referring to the receiver, the one that gets broadcasts from radio stations. It was too noisy, and he wanted to holler for his copilot. He was alone and it's hard to control a plane under those conditions. The copilot didn't come.

I don't see fire in the engine. I just see that it's not working. It's dead. Consequently, the first thing the pilot did was to look for the opportunity to make an emergency landing as quickly as possible. He was losing altitude very rapidly. The plane did this, more or less. (He draws the route taken by the plane, but admits his calculation of distances might be wrong.) The pilot, being a man with an extraordinary visual memory, knew that on a southwesterly course he would find a place where he could make a forced landing.

To reach that place he would have to pass between two mountains peaks—that really look like three. I don't want to analyze that too much. Anyway, he couldn't sneak between them. He had to keep turning. But he couldn't turn to his right at any time because of his dead engine. If he should try, he'd go into a nose dive. That's why he kept flying in a wide-open spiral.

I talked about this in my first communication with the people in Uruguay. I explained the maneuver which the pilot made, using sketch A2. Now, if you take sketch A2, and follow it from right to left, you collide with the first mountain, which has a flattened summit. Between this one and the next one—with a cone-shaped peak—there's a pass, a canyon. That's where the pilot wanted to go—toward the ocean on a southwesterly direction. He couldn't make it. So he kept circling, passing over the lake and rounding the rock or small mountain, which is in the middle of the lake.

After circling that mountain, he crashed into the third mountain—the highest one—the one with the chopped-off peak [volcano]. Its slope goes down to the lake. But look here! There's a huge cavity near the base and THAT'S WHERE THE PLANE IS. It can't be seen from the air. The only way you can see the plane is from the level of the lake. The tail probably. The pilot tried to glide over the lake, but couldn't. That ceiling of rock got in his way.

IBANEZ: Can you give me the location of the mountain, the lake, the huge rock, et cetera—indicating north, south, east, and west?

CROISSET: Yes I can. The airplane was coming from northeast to southwest. When I come in this direction and see the lake, the edge nearest me has a strip of sand. I can see it perfectly because there are no high mountains in front of me. Here, near that sandy beach, I see something that prohibits passage—a house—a lettered sign—indicating danger. I've already told you this lake is well-known.

IBANEZ: Then why is that danger sign on the other side—near the beach—rather than here?

CROISSET: Well, that's because the only passage to this canyon or grotto is near the beach. They go around the lake—not across it. And they always approach from the northeast.

It's extremely difficult for an airplane to reach this location, for the simple reason that, once it descends to the level of the lake, it can't regain enough altitude. The pilot's maneuver around the rock in the center of the lake was not a capricious one. Going south, passing that rock on his left side, he couldn't have gone far without smashing into the mountains on the southern margin of the lake. He had no alternative but to circle the rock. In the summertime that rock looks huge—like a small mountain. Now, let me talk more about the lake. It's important. How high is it? I don't know. They told me it was snowing there, and that confuses me. Snow can be very deceiving—making it difficult to calculate distances. It makes everything look uniform.

But the pilot knew where he was flying. He was a man with a great visual memory; so he knew that passing between those two mountains he would reach the ocean. He knew that route, knew that he would pass over a familiar area before reaching the coast.

IBANEZ: That is awfully vague, Mr. Croisset. There must be many well-known places between the cordillera and the ocean. The area is enormous.

CROISSET: You must remember that I'm Dutch, and that I can't easily adapt myself to dimensions outside Holland. When I look at a map I see it as a Dutchman, and I might possibly commit errors in calculating distances. But one thing that's certain is that the pilot wanted to go southwest so as to find level ground for a forced landing. And through that route there's a place that reminds me of *The Alamo*—the movie. Did you see it?

IBANEZ: Coming from which direction?

CROISSET: From the plane's original route. And before reaching the lake there's this abandoned old mine, which is on the left side. I think that's all. There is nothing more. If I give more details the confusion will be worse. No one will see it clearly then.

IBANEZ: Can you tell me more about the plane itself?

CROISSET: The plane is below that mountain with the flattened peak. My problem is determining whether it's in the lake or on the mountain slope. It could be in the water and at the base of the mountain. I always see it there. It can't be seen from the air. I have no contact with the plane. I mean that I don't see—or feel—any signs of life in the plane. The nose of the plane is demolished, and the wings are torn off. I don't see the left engine. Perhaps he lost it. I don't know. There's an emergency exit on the left side that's partly open, but not all the way. It could have been knocked halfway open by the crash. It's not the door to the cabin—the cockpit is completely smashed. I see no one at the windows. At any rate, I can only say that I see no sign of life in the plane.

IBANEZ: Can you tell me something about the pilot—in a personal sense?

CROISSET: I've seen all this through the eyes of the pilot. One doesn't pay much attention to one's self under such circumstances. That's why I can't give many details about the pilot. What I *can* say is that he always opened his shirt collar and loosened his tie when he took his seat in the cockpit. I can also tell you that he wore his watch loose on his wrist—very loose.

I can't give you more personal details about the pilot because he was completely absorbed in the emergency that faced him. He was the first one to realize the danger they were in. All the responsibility for the passengers and crew was his.

IBANEZ: Logically. Now, sir, in accordance with your vision of the accident, the pilot died.

CROISSET: Yes—I think so.

IBANEZ: If you have seen all this through the eyes of the pilot and were more in contact with him than you were with the other occupants of the plane, didn't you feel in some special way the impact and eventual death of the pilot?

CROISSET: You can't imagine the emptiness one feels just seconds before an accident like this. Think of how you feel when your car slides or skates across any icy stretch of road. All you feel is a vacuum. You're not even thinking. It's only a matter of seconds and then . . . BAM! It's over.

Prior to the foregoing session between Croisset and Ibanez on December 15, Carlos Paez, Sr., exchanged at least fifteen long-distance telephone conversations with the Dutch clairvoyant; and during one of their extended talks, Croisset had said, "I see a cross near the plane—a large cross in the snow."

Hearing this, Paez once again felt great hope and hurriedly organized another expedition into the snow-covered mountains, receiving considerable support from most of the other parents. "That cross is a sure sign!" he kept telling them. But soon thereafter, a team of geologists revealed that they had made a cross in the snow in the same area. Undaunted and refusing to give up, Paez insisted that it was nonetheless "a good omen" —that the difficulties would soon be resolved.

Although certain skeptics were tempted to point out that Croisset could have got most of his purportedly astonishing "revelations" by simply reading back issues of *El Mercurio* (Chile's most comprehensive daily newspaper), they decided to keep mum when Paez was around, unwilling to dampen his spirits.

One is reminded that Bishop James A. Pike consulted a clairvoyant named Rev. Arthur Ford, who told the controversial clergymen that he could be "put in touch" with his son, who had committed suicide a couple of years earlier. In a subsequent seance conducted by Rev. Ford, the bishop allegedly spoke to his dead son, and later said that "through his occult powers Reverend Ford revealed certain matters that were quite personal to me"—the *nickname* of a colleague who had died many years before, and certain other little-known personal details about fellow churchmen and friends who were no longer living. Thus, he was sure that Ford had amazing psychic powers and extrasensory perception, that he could indeed communicate with the dead. But in a later book about Ford, *The Man Who Talked with the Dead,* it was revealed that the clairvoyant had always amassed numerous newspaper clippings to ascertain personal data on prospective clients. He had, in fact, carefully read and memorized the *New York Times* obituaries of some of Bishop Pike's well-known friends and colleagues, and many of the "personal details" that so astonished the bishop were to be found in the news clippings—one of which mentioned the supposedly private nickname.

But even if he had been informed that Gerard Croisset had employed the same techniques in acquiring information about the accident and its victims, Carlos Paez would have most likely remained convinced that he was right about the plane's location. "My son is alive!" he would tell everyone, with dogged conviction. "And his friends are alive. So I'll keep searching until I find them." But the stubbornly optimistic painter seemed to ignore Croisset's statement that he could see no signs of life inside the fuselage.

But since all the passengers and crew members were assumed to be dead, the continuing search efforts by their parents and relatives received little or no publicity after the first few weeks. Consequently, the survivors heard no mention of themselves on the radio newscasts they listened to almost every morning, except for a brief notice about a special funeral mass for the members of the Old Christian rugby team, which led to a few bitter comments.

"When people think you're dead, you actually begin to feel dead," said Alfredo Delgado, on a gloomy afternoon in late November. "I've been a corpse for six weeks now, and it's beginning to show."

"But there are certain advantages to all this," observed a more cheerful companion. "Perhaps this will make you a more compassionate lawyer or judge, Alfredo."

"Or a little callous," said a third man. "And possibly indifferent to death or suffering. We've seen so much of it up here that I can't react to it anymore. I guess I've lost all my feelings."

He was probably referring to the person who had died shortly after Numa Turcatti allowed himself to die of starvation by refusing to eat the flesh of his dead companions. The number of survivors was thus reduced to sixteen. All of them, with the exception of Roy Harley, were free of any serious illness and about as healthy as could be expected under the circumstances. And though most of them were noticeably gaunt, they were strong enough to perform modest chores around the "camp" and participate in the now-more-frequent "expeditions for a way out." Harley, however, was apparently suffering from severe malnutrition. Like Turcatti, he had initially refused to eat the meat pellets, but he was later persuaded to take them. Nevertheless, he was occasionally seen wandering away from the cabin to some private place where he could quietly give up the meal he had just eaten.

As for their psychological health, most of the young men seemed to remain on a fairly even keel in spite of periodic spells of deep depression. Ironically, some of their "sudden glooms" were brought on by one of the games they played to shake off the boredom that developed whenever they were cooped up by bad weather. This particular game was called *A la verdad*, which is the equivalent of "Truth or Consequences."

Considering the complex emotional problems each was experiencing—the trauma of the plane accident, the incipient starvation, dizzy spells from lack of oxygen, the fatal avalanche and constant fear of another, the often hideous death of relatives and close friends, their forced imprisonment inside the narrow smelly fuselage, the sense of isolation in the barren frozen cordillera, the guilt of survival when others had died or were dying, the continuously-smashed hopes of being rescued, their strong unyielding Catholic sense of sin, and, perhaps most painful of all, their consumption of human flesh—considering all this, could they safely risk the hazards of a game like *A la verdad?* (In the words of a prominent New York psychoanalyst, Dr. Mildred Lerner, "Those men were certainly asking for trouble when they played that game—but it could also be healthily cathartic.")

Undoubtedly aware of the emotional risks—and perhaps inwardly driven to *do penance* in one form or another—they played the game frequently and were often angered or saddened by some of the questions they had to answer. "It was like confessing your sins," Carlos

Paez, Jr., later explained. "But instead of whispering them to a priest in a private booth, we confessed them out loud and said things we had never said before— things that were awfully painful to admit, or even to think about."

"Was it some form of exorcism?" someone asked, obviously referring to the eating of human flesh.

"No—not at all. There was no need to purify ourselves. We had no sense of sinning in that respect. Anyone would understand that we *had* to do that, anyone who had read about certain things that happened during World War II."*

Thus, except for a few oblique references (always in the vaguest of terms), there was no talk about their daily intake of proteins. Finally, however, their unavoidable awareness of the strips of meat dangling from the ceiling of the fuselage would lead to moments of cathartic black humor—allusions to "poor Yorick," for example, or playful variations on the names of dishes served at the favorite restaurants they so often discussed. Nevertheless, the subject of food was seldom broached when they played *A la verdad*.

Yet they willingly bared themselves to questions they might have avoided under different circumstances, talking bluntly to each other like soldiers in an army camp just before a major maneuver, or like strangers on a long train ride who talk freely and frankly because they'll never see each other again. Most of these questions were treated with often-embarrassing candor and occasional whiffs of masculine humor. Nevertheless, a few topics were not included in their Game of Truth. No one, for example, would dare inquire about a man's sexual relations with his wife or fiancee. In this regard, they were remaining completely consistent with the average Latino's *macho* attitudes toward sex. Believing that sex is somehow dirty or sinful, they insist that their fiancees be virgins and their wives virginal, and there-

* A group of American soldiers, stranded in the South Pacific, had engaged in cannibalism to keep from starving.

fore not subject to any "sordid" speculations about
sex. One of them later told reporters, "Of course, we
talked about our girl friends and fiancees—but always
with great respect." They would feel no such inhibi-
tions in discussions about their mistresses or one-night
girl friends.

And what if someone should obliquely hint that a
man's fiancee (or wife) might not remain faithful now
that he was presumed dead? That would indeed be
dangerous and could easily lead to violence. Some
Latinos are so obsessed with virginity that they have
been known to break an engagement if they themselves
have gone to bed with their fiancees—on the supposi-
tion that, "If she's willing to sleep with me before mar-
riage, she may also have done it with someone else."

Though apparently not prompted by such inflamma-
tory scrutiny, there were moments of strain among some
of the sixteen survivors and even a few fist fights. In
mid-November, Carlos Paez got into a brief brawl with
Roberto Canessa, swarming over the slimmer medical
student with both fists flailing to head and body; but
when they were finally pulled apart, neither of them
could remember (or cared to remember) why they had
started fighting. And after looking at each other with
puzzled expressions, they fell into each other's arms,
tearfully swearing never to lose their tempers again.
But a week or so later, just before the evening prayers,
Paez and Antonio Vicintin squared off for a fight in-
stigated by a casual teasing insult—an insult that later
seemed so ludicrous they both went into spasms of
laughter. "I guess I'd gotten so tense I would have shot
someone if he'd merely forgotten to say 'Good morning'
or something equally trivial," Vicintin later explained.

As one of the acknowledged leaders of the group,
Parrado frequently served as a moderator between the
disputants and generally advised them to take a long
hike up the mountain whenever they felt too much
tension building inside themselves.

The evening prayers also had a calming effect, and
served to bolster their hopes during sieges of deep

depression. "All this praying is new to me," Paez admitted one evening. "I've always believed in God and the Virgin Maria, but I'd quit going to communion—or even to mass—but I've suddenly changed here in the cordillera." His mother had given him a rosary just before he boarded the F-27 in Montevideo, and he had later found it in his shirt pocket. But he and some of the other survivors had forgotten how to pray with a rosary and had to learn all over again. "I'm sure glad the priests and nuns at the colegio aren't around to see how careless we've become," one man told Parrado. "They'd make us do triple penance."

Emotionally shaken by the deaths of their dearest relatives and friends and by their own miraculous escape, even the most "lapsed" Catholics became extremely devout as the days became weeks and the weeks became months. Paez was especially affected by the death of Rafael Vasco Etchevarren, a friend who had suffered a severe injury to his right leg in the crash. With the fractured bone protruding through a deep gash that refused to heal, Rafael had stubbornly refused to give in. Then, when the avalanche struck sixteen days later, he was completely buried under the snow and Paez had to bring him back to life with mouth-to-mouth resuscitation. Thereafter his health wavered from poor to critical, Paez frequently serving as attending nurse. "It's my fault that he's here," he told Canessa one afternoon. "I was the one who begged him to come with us when there were only three seats left on the plane. So I'm really to blame." Finally, after six weeks of struggling to stay alive, Rafael was stricken with a pulmonary congestion, and his legs stiffened as if suddenly frozen. Paez knew he was dying because he had become delirious. "We had seen many of them die, so we knew what to expect. First, they would rapidly get weaker and weaker. Then there would be two days of delirium, when they would say all kinds of strange and incoherent things, often imagining themselves to be somewhere else—on the beach at Carasco or at a park in Montevideo. And on the third day they would die." Thus, knowing that his friend was about to succumb, Paez kneeled next to Rafael's pallet on the cold floor of the cabin and asked him to pray. *Rezamos un Padre Nuestro y un Ave Maria, y fueron sus unicos momentos de lucidez.* "We said the Lord's Prayer and a Hail Mary, and those were his only lucid moments." The same night he died.

"It was awful to see our best friends dying," Paez later told his father. "And it frightened us to think we might die the same way. We weren't afraid of a spiritual death because we knew our souls would be with God. But we *were* afraid of physical death."

And feeding that fear was the continuing presence of death itself—the snow-covered bodies lying just outside the cabin, the strips of meat hanging from the rafters, the too-easily-remembered moans of dying companions which still seemed to echo inside the cramped walls of the battered fuselage. These awesome reminders were all the more terrifying after dark, when the nightly bull sessions had ended and each man was left with his own thoughts, his own painful memories.

As for Fernando Parrado, the long, cold nights must have reminded him of his mother and sister dying, the numb frustrating hopelessness he had felt as they died in his arms. Lying there in the gloomy darkness of their never comfortable dormitory, listening to the deep sighs and occasional muffled sobbing of his friends, he probably remembered Susana reaching for the rugby ball as it bounced down the aisle of the plane and giggling when it grazed her shoulder on a rebound; his mother probably fingering her rosary as the plane bounced through a down draught just after taking off from Mendoza; the smile on his father's face as he waved goodbye at the airport in Montevideo. And drifting further back, before the accident, he might have remembered the suntanned bodies on a crowded beach as he sped along the coast highway on his Suzuki motorcycle, or a pretty mini-skirted girl buying a peach from the pedlar across the street from Otto's. But inevitably, through such a montage of remembered faces and places, his mind's eye would probably catch the stark image of snow-capped graves and the looming silhouette of El Tinguiririca, eerily beautiful in the waning light of another day. Or there might have been a lingering close-up of a desecrated grave, an always startling reminder of the most difficult decision any of them had ever made or would be likely to make ever again.

But assuming they should finally be rescued, how would they explain that decision to their families, their friends, and to the families of those whose bodies had been sacrificed? And would they finally be able to forgive themselves for having violated that most ancient of taboos? In a moment of tormented reflection, one of Parrado's friends had said, "Those who have died have become a part of us, and they shall always be with us."

Though there is no way of knowing, he may have been thinking of Sir James Frazer's classic treatise on magic and religion, *The Golden Bough,* and more specifically about the following passage from the chapter titled "Homeopathic Magic of a Flesh Diet":

. . . The flesh and blood of dead men are commonly eaten and drunk to inspire bravery, wisdom, or other qualities for which the men themselves were remarkable, or which are supposed to have their special seat in the particular part eaten. Thus among the mountain tribes of South-Eastern Africa there are ceremonies by which the youths are formed into guilds or lodges, and among the rites of initiation there is one which is intended to infuse courage, intelligence, and other qualities into the novices. Whenever an enemy who has behaved with conspicuous bravery is killed, his liver, which is considered the seat of valour; his ears, which are supposed to be the seat of intelligence; the skin of his forehead, which is regarded as the seat of perseverance; his testicles, which are held to be the seat of strength; and other members, which are viewed as the seat of other virtues, are cut from his body and baked to cinders. The ashes are care-

fully kept in the horn of a bull, and, during the
ceremonies observed at circumcision, are mixed
with other ingredients into a kind of paste, which
is administered by the tribal priest to the youths.
By this means the strength, valour, intelligence,
and other virtues of the slain are believed to be
imparted to the eaters. When Basutos of the mountains have killed a very brave foe, they immediately cut out his heart and eat it, because this is
supposed to give them his courage and strength in
battle. . . .

But Parrado and his fellow survivors would find no
comfort in such bizarre superstitions. Theirs had been
an act of survival, a pragmatic and medically rational
decision to obtain the proteins necessary to stay alive.
No attempt had been made to find some mystical rationale for doing what had to be done. Still, in the final
analysis, they might eventually have to search beyond
the realm of pure reason and hard logic for a more
profound and emotionally acceptable justification.

Meanwhile, a more immediate, more pressing problem faced them: How would they get out of their frozen
prison before the spring thaw and the numerous avalanches that were sure to come, possibly pushing the
down-slanted fuselage over the precipice and into the
steep canyon below? There had already been huge
slides on an adjacent slope, monstrous masses of snow
rumbling onto the still-frozen lake. Time was running
short. They had to take action—and soon.

"We've got to have another conference," Parrado
said to Canessa one afternoon in early December.
"There's trouble ahead."

"How about this evening?" suggested Canessa. "Right
after our prayers."

"The sooner the better, Roberto."

That same night, after a prolonged discussion that
was more spirited than controversial, it was unanimous-
ly agreed that three men would launch what Parrado
called "a journey to the end"—that they would keep

going until they reached someone who would rescue those who stayed behind.

"We're going for broke this time," he said, pressing the nose-piece of his thick-lensed eyeglasses. "We're not turning back."

"Who's going with you?" asked Sabella, apparently assuming that Parrado would lead the expedition.

"Canessa for sure—because we may need a doctor. And someone who's in fairly good physical shape."

"I'm your man," said Antonio Vicintin, clownishly flexing his muscles. "I'm ready to climb a hundred mountains."

There were several other volunteers, but Vicintin was finally selected as the third man. They set December 10 as the day of departure, and planned to take along enough rations for at least twenty days. Parrado, Canessa, and Vicintin were also "ordered" to eat double rations and to perform special muscle-building exercises for at least four days before they left.

"We'll give you a day of rest before you take off," said Delgado. "But no goofing off before then."

Since no one in the group had ever done any serious mountain climbing, they had only a vague notion of what kind of equipment would be needed, but they managed to devise snowshoes from seat cushions or aluminum slats; sleeping bags with foam-rubber lining torn from the plane's refrigeration unit; knapsack bindings from seat belts, which could also be converted into climbing ropes; hooks fashioned out of broken rods from the pilot's cabin; and extra "blankets" previously patched together from seat covers. It was a team effort, with everyone doing his share.

Finally, on the evening before their departure, special prayers were offered for the trio's safety and well-being. And because they would be leaving before dawn, with little time for farewells, their thirteen friends gathered to give them warm affectionate *abrazos*. His friends later recalled the pensive look on Parrado's face as he wandered through the barely visible graves near the cabin just before they crawled into their pallets. Some

of the graves were empty now, and soon others would
be empty.

The women would be last. Thus, as the weeks had
slipped by with little hope of rescue, Parrado must have
wondered if they would eventually sacrifice his own
mother and sister, whose stiff frozen bodies lay buried
in the mounds of snow nearby, in the improvised refrigerator where they had lain for sixty days. ("Take
good care of them," his father had said. "I leave them
in your charge.") Needless to say, he could never have
brought himself to touch even the slightest portion of
their bodies. But what of the others, his fellow survivors? Had there not been an implicit—if not explicit
—understanding that eventually they might have to
consume the flesh of everyone who had died? Indeed
some of his *companeros* had already seen the sacrifice
of their dearest, oldest friends.

Pondering this darkest of all dilemmas, Parrado must
have felt an unbearable anguish, an agonizing help-
lessness as he made final preparations to leave the
camp. One can well imagine the tall, gaunt youngster
standing by the graves, staring hard at the jagged, snow-
capped peaks all around him, his jaws clamped in utter
frustration, tears probably brimming in his eyes. Even
the strongest of men would have wept at least inwardly
had they faced such a dilemma.

His companions obviously realized (though they may
not have mentioned it) that Nando was probably
troubled by the nightmare possibility that his mother
and sister might eventually be sacrificed as all the
others had. Indeed, one of them later hinted that he had
quickly volunteered to lead the expedition because he
didn't want to be present if that grim prospect should
finally come to pass.

But Parrado showed no signs of emotional stress
when he woke up at four the next morning and quickly
roused Canessa and Vicintin. "Let's get moving," he
said. "It will soon be daybreak."

Packing their gear in less then ten minutes, they
crept out of the cabin like cautious burglars, whispering

adios to the few still-drowsy *companeros* who had gotten up to bid them *buen viaje*. Outside it was still dark and bone-freezing cold, a sharp wind instantly numbing their faces as they started down the now familiar slope toward the frozen lake. Moving cautiously but with all possible haste, they reached the base as dawn broke across the entire cordillera, a dazzling shimmer of light and shadow that would have tied the tongue of even the most articulate poet.

"Look at that beautiful damned mountain!" exclaimed Vicintin, staring at the towering splendor of El Tinguiririca.

"It will seem more damned than beautiful when we start climbing it," said Parrado.

Since they had no idea where they were, they could not have known that the mountain was the dead volcano known as El Tinguiririca, that it was among the highest peaks in the entire Andes—more than twenty-two thousand feet (or four miles) above sea level, and that only a very few highly skilled and courageous mountain climbers had ever scaled its summit.

"Why don't we go around it?" said Vicintin. "I know it's due west, but a straight line isn't always the best way to go. Not even for crows, Fernando."

"Well, it's the highest peak around here, Antonio, and from the summit we'll be able to get a much better view of what lies ahead. We might possibly see the Pacific Ocean."

"Or at least that town called Curico," added Canessa. "The one the pilot mentioned as he started his descent."

"I think it's in a valley," said Parrado. "In this beautiful long valley that stretches between the cordillera and the coast range."

"Let's get going, then," Vincintin urged. "I'm anxious to see anything that's green. All this snow is beginning to bore me."

"Take your time," Parrado cautioned. "It's going to be a long, hard climb to the top, and it may be pretty icy up there."

Making their way through high drifts of snow and

talking only when necessary as they walked single file with Parrado in the lead, they reached the base of the volcano at midmorning. Then, after a brief rest, they started their ascent, searching for spots where the winds had blown off the snow to provide secure footing, or reaching through layers of snow for bare rock that could serve as an anchor for their hand-crafted climbing hooks. Probe, hook, and climb, slipping now and then on an icy surface, and once again probing for a safer foothold. Hour after hour of slow, muscle-straining progress through devious crevices and abrupt ledges hidden by snow that was mushy here and frozen there. With the sun getting warm, they could feel sweat oozing from their faces, armpits, chests, and legs, a pleasant sensation after the chilling numbness of the early morning. But they were finding it a bit harder to breathe, gasping now and then when exerting extra effort to scale a more difficult boulder.

Just before sundown, more than fourteen hours after their departure, they found a small ledge with an overhanging rock formation. "This looks like a good place," said Canessa, breathing heavily and wiping his brow. "But we'll have to get rid of some of this snow."

Fifteen minutes later, after clearing most of the snow off the shelf, they settled down for a rest, their aching backs slouched against the cliff. Almost directly in front of them across the invisible lake, they could see the wingless fuselage of the F-27 and several insect-sized figures probably waving goodnight as the waning sun suddenly disappeared and left everything in darkness.

Shivering as the temperature dropped twenty or thirty degrees within an hour, Parrado suggested they huddle together like three snails in a single shell. "It's going to be an awfully cold night, especially after all the sweating we've done."

"I've already got icicles hanging from my armpits," said Vicintin through chattering teeth. "And they're beginning to tickle."

Snuggling body-to-body and periodically massaging

one another's arms and legs, they tried to sleep in three shifts, one man staying awake to guard against all of them falling asleep and freezing to death. The "stay-awaker" would manipulate and massage his partners' limbs to keep them from getting stiff or numb. None of them slept well, but they managed to ease some of the weariness out of their swollen muscles and by sunrise they were ready to climb again.

Clawing their way from one ledge to another, occasionally slipping back when their hooks failed to hold or when their rugby shoes couldn't gain sufficient traction on an icy surface, they climbed higher and higher and felt the air getting thinner and more difficult to inhale. Their lungs were near to bursting and their knees increasingly wobbly from strains far greater than they had ever experienced in a rugby match, forcing them to rest more frequently than the day before.

"I've never in my life felt so tired," Vicintin confessed when they took a break to eat their noon rations. "My legs feel like rubber."

"We'll rest for a half hour," said Parrado, slumping against a flat rock. "Then we'll try for the top by sundown."

But the summits of certain mountains have a capricious way of receding and often trick the eye, especially when covered with snow. So they were still some distance from the top when nightfall forced them to quit. Having found another niche, another cracked lip on the face of the mountain, they took off their backpacks and made themselves as comfortable as possible. Far below them, perhaps a mile lower, they could still see the vague outline of the amputated plane, but their friends were no more than grains of pepper or perhaps not visible at all. Too exhausted to talk in more than simple sentences and putatively responsive grunts and sighs, they huddled together and wearily massaged each other as a cold wind meanly sliced at their cramped bodies.

Their fingers too chilled to handle the ebony beads of a rosary, they said a *Padre Nuestro* and an *Ave Maria,* praying with a fervor that seemed to challenge

the cold. Though not too successfully. Afterward, while
the others dozed and squirmed in utter fatigue, Parrado
took the first four-hour watch and kept himself awake
by periodically pinching himself. The stars were chips
of ice spread across a sky as blue-black dark as the
morning they started, reminding him of the last words
he had said on leaving camp: "May God help us. Because if we don't return for you, then you'll know that
we've died on the way." Keenly aware of the pitfalls
they had just barely avoided in the past two days, the
snow-concealed traps all along the way, the steep crevices and slippery narrow ledges, he realized that his
words had not been mere rhetoric, that they could easily
be killed in a false move or possibly freeze to death on
a high ledge from which they could neither advance
nor retreat. It was a kind of Russian roulette at every
step. Still, he felt a current of "survival luck" pulsing
through him, through all the sixteen who were still living. He himself had certainly defied all the odds when
he snapped out of his three-day coma with no more
physical complications than someone who had simply
taken a long nap. Canessa had told him it was a miracle.
Having survived all that, he had no fear of whatever
dangers might lie ahead. Nor any fear of death itself.

Progress on the third day was slower and more
hazardous than before, the thin cold air piercing their
lungs like slivers of ice as they climbed higher and
higher. Lacking proper ropes and secure hooks, they
had to claw their way with numb, bleeding hands and
bruised elbows and knees, clutching the edge of a rock
overhead and pulling themselves up and over with
desperate spurts of energy, then flopping belly-down on
the ledge they had just reached, trembling with exhaustion and gasping for air. Finally, at midafternoon, while
still short of their goal, Canessa and Vicintin had to
call it a day.

"I can't move another step," said Canessa. "I'm
ready to cave in, Fernando."

"Same here," said Vicintin, his head drooping.

"I understand," said Parrado. "You really look beat.

Both of you stay right here, and I'll go ahead. I can see the top now."

Forcing himself to ignore the pulsating aches in every muscle of his lean body, he crawled and struggled the last two hundred yards to the summit. It was then that he realized that the mountain was really a dead volcano; and, circling the rim to stand on the western fringe, he also realized that there were still other mountains to cross and that the ocean was not yet in sight—nor was the green valley he had hoped to see. Near the base of the northern slope of the volcano, he saw a dark strip that might be a highway or railroad line; but it would require too much of a detour to find out. They had to keep moving west, across an area that was awesome in its ethereal splendor and frustrating in its vast dimensions. Far, far below him, beyond the jagged ridge of the next range of mountains, he could see the dark outline of a forest—or perhaps it was merely the shadow of a huge canyon. It was so difficult to see the real shape of things, and to judge their actual size, when they were covered with snow—so he dared not become too hopeful; yet there was an undeniable surge in his pulse when he saw the dark mass.

Scrambling down the icy slope to where he had left Canessa and Vicintin, temporarily forgetting how tired he was, Parrado gave them a quick report on what he had seen from the summit. "We've still got a long way to go. It could take us another ten days to reach anyone, and I'm afraid our rations won't last that long."

"Any suggestions, Fernando?"

"Just one, Roberto," he answered. "I think one of us will have to go back, so we can stretch the rations a little further. And I guess it should be Antonio. I've got more accustomed to these altitudes than either of you, so I'm choosing myself. And we may need your medical skills, Roberto."

Though reluctant to leave the expedition, Vicintin had to accept Parrado's logic. "I'd like to stay with you," he said, "but I see your point, Nando. I'll go back tomorrow."

"*Bueno,* Antonio—but there's something else I want to mention. I think—though I really can't be sure—but, anyway, I think I saw a dark line that may be a highway or railroad track. It's way down on the northern base of this mountain. Just a dark line that curves a little through what looks like a narrow valley."

"Why don't we check it tomorrow?"

"Because it might be nothing, and we can't afford to lose any time or energy finding out. We've got to keep pushing toward the west," said Parrado. "But if you don't hear from us in ten or twelve days, you might consider leading an expedition in that direction."

Having thus resolved the potentially touchy problem of deflating Antonio's ego, they settled in for the night, once again nestling close to each other for body warmth. But a restful sleep was impossible at that high altitude, about twenty-two thousand feet above sea level. Finding it difficult to breathe and plagued with dizzy spells, they were awake most of the night. Still tired but nevertheless anxious to get underway, they dragged themselves to their feet at sunrise and quickly tied on their backpacks.

"See you soon," said Vicintin before the others left. "And may God be with you."

His eyes still on them as they disappeared from sight, he finally turned to look at the sun spreading a radiant golden light across the entire cordillera. Five minutes later he started down the eastern slope of the volcano, slowly at first, picking his way with great care. But when he suddenly spotted a long narrow strip of snow that looked like a ski run, his caution fled. Joining the two foam-rubber cushions that he had been using as snowshoes, Vicintin made himself a toboggan. Then, after making the sign of the Cross and mumbling a quick prayer, he hopped on his cushions and zoomed down the slope at an exhilarating pace, yelling "*Ole! Ole!*" as he picked up speed. Whooshing to a sudden stop when he crashed into a huge snowdrift, he picked himself up and soon found another toboggan slide. Down and down he went, locating one slide after another, until he finally got to the bottom—*less than forty-five minutes after he had started.* Three days to the top, and less than one hour to come down.

He got back to the fuselage two hours later, and immediately explained why he had returned. "They've got a long, long way to go," he said with a hint of tears in his dark eyes. "So they needed my share of the rations. They'll also need all our prayers. And lots of luck."

V

Beyond El Tinguiririca

Pausing to rest on the summit of the volcano, their eyes scanning the jumble of snow-crowned peaks that spread westward till they merged with a gray mass of low clouds, Parrado and Canessa spent a half hour discussing possible routes to the valley of Curico.

"That looks like a fairly good pass," said Parrado, pointing toward a spot where two mountains merged at mid-slope.

"But the snow looks pretty deep there, Nando, and that incline is rather steep. I'd rather try this other side —through that low wedge that seems to dip into a valley or canyon."

"That does look better. Safer, too. And maybe we'll get there by sunset."

After taking another long look at the various peaks directly in front of them, as if to engrave on the inner eye a detailed map of the jagged contours, they began their descent from Tinguiririca. They crawled ass-backward over some boulders, allowed themselves to slide down a few slippery grades, sometimes jumped from one ledge to another, teetering on the edge of an icy precipice now and then, generally making much faster progress and breathing more easily than they had during the previous three days. But they were constantly aware of danger all along the way—narrow gaps concealed by snow, knife-sharp rocks, and huge masses of snow poised for an avalanche at any moment. Even a loose stone could cause a twisted ankle, a mere sprain that could nevertheless halt their progress for several days. Long enough for an injured man to starve or freeze to death.

Now in their fourth day of unimaginable fatigue, Parrado was beginning to sense still another danger— perhaps the most insidious one. Aside from distorting all dimensions, he found that the snow had a mesmerizing, almost narcotic quality, that it induced a certain lassitude, "a desire to sleep forever and ever." (In his classic story of an aviator similarly trapped in the Andes, *Terre des Hommes,* Antoine de Saint-Exupery quotes him as saying: "In the snow a man loses his instinct for self-preservation. All he wants to do is sleep.") Increasingly aware of this mesmeric threat, Parrado warned Canessa against falling asleep whenever they stopped for a ten-minute break—usually every two hours.

"Try to keep your eyes open, Roberto. And fight it off. Don't give in."

"I've been trying, Nando. But even as we're plowing through the snow, I keep wanting to close them—if only for a few seconds. Just close my eyes and blot out everything."

"I know, Roberto. But we can't give in. We've got to keep our eyes open."

But when he himself stumbled into the soft caressing snow later in the day, he must have felt like a boxer who has been knocked to the canvas for the third time in the fourteenth round, no longer feeling anything and barely hearing the referee counting to ten. Closing his eyes, Parrado could be rid of the mountains, the sky, the snow, and all the aches in his worn-out limbs—but there was Canessa leaning over him, pulling him to his feet and telling him to keep his eyes open. ("Come on, Nando, get up. We've got to keep moving.")

Thus realizing there was "bad sleep" as well as "good sleep," they were all the more determined to avoid dozing off during the day and to spell each other at night so that one of them would always be awake. It could have been fatal, especially in freezing temperatures, for both of them to fall asleep at once. In fact, the cold itself also had a narcotic, desensitizing effect. As Saint-Exupery says of his hero in *Terre des Hommes,* "You began to love that freezing cold which had become a drug resembling morphine that overwhelmed you with an exquisite peace."

Resisting the dual drugs of snow and cold, Parrado took the first watch that fourth night and kept himself awake with small tasks—massaging Canessa's arms and legs, then massaging his own, tightening the knots of their climbing "ropes," made with seat belts, retying his shoelaces, periodically snuggling against his partner to create and preserve body warmth, then doing something else to keep busy. His mind was also occupied with plans for the next day's journey, speculating on alternative routes if a previously chosen one should come to a dead end because of an impassable canyon or perhaps an avalanche. But, inevitably, his thoughts would drift to less immediate concerns. He might start thinking about his mother and sister lying in that row of frozen graves near the plane; about his father sitting terribly alone in their big house at Punta Gorda; about Turcatti refusing to eat and starving to death; the pilot saying something about a place called Curico as he descended through soup-thick clouds, someone yelling, *"DIOS MIO! DIOS MIO! DIOS MIO!";* then a series of brain-stunning jolts as the F-27 was torn apart; and the long period of nothingness when he lay in a coma, first taken for dead, then dragging himself to the wrecked fuselage before passing out again. Crystal-hard images smudged by a fatigued brain, and Parrado pinching himself to stay awake. Then, thank God, Canessa saying, "Go to sleep, Nando—I'm awake now."

Four hours later, Parrado was on his feet again, doing a few exercises to work the cramps out of his body and dabbing his bearded face with snow. Soon they were on the march again, the early sun projecting their elongated shadows on the snow ahead of them as they crossed a narrow valley and began climbing the next mountain. The fifth day would be like the one before, except for an afternoon snowstorm that slowed their progress. But their spirits were not dampened, because an hour earlier they had seen a bird (a hawk, perhaps) flying near the crest of a distant mountain.

"We're getting close!" Canessa had yelled. "That's the first living thing we've seen in two months."

"Macanudo, che," Parrado had said, not wanting to become too optimistic. "But it's still a long way off."

They were now crossing a range lower than Tinguiririca, and consequently could breathe more easily, but the night was almost as cold as the previous ones. Once again taking the first watch, Parrado tucked their bottle of drinking water inside his shirt, for if the bottle were left exposed, the liquid would soon freeze and crack the glass, leaving only snow to quench their thirst. And that, they both knew, would cause severe cramps. With the bottle still tucked inside his shirt as if it were a fuzzy teddy bear, Parrado instantly fell asleep.

On the following morning, after a series of wake-up exercises to shake the kinks out of their bodies, they started crossing a frozen, snow-covered lake on which someone had apparently trampled through the snow to make a couple of furrows that intersected in the middle. Judging from their subsequent talks with other persons, one can imaginatively reconstruct the conversations between Parrado and Canessa when they saw the intersecting furrows and as they struggled through the frozen cordillera during the remainder of their long trek.

"Looks as if somebody's made a cross here—like the one we made to signal the planes," said Canessa, with a puzzled frown.

"It sure does," answered Parrado, scanning the surrounding mountains for signs of another crashed plane. "That certainly looks like a distress signal. But I don't see anything that looks like a plane."*

"Maybe some animals made it—a deer or some other mountain animal."

"I doubt it," said Parrado. "Why would animals make such straight lines?"

The cross was still on their minds as they began climbing the mountain just beyond the lake.

"I'm sure of one thing," said Canessa, looking back at it. "It was made fairly recently. Otherwise the snows and the winds would have covered it over."

"But there's been less snow at this lower altitude, a lot less. And it's a bit warmer."

"I'd say *much* warmer. In fact, it's getting too warm for comfort."

With the sun beating down on them as they struggled from one ledge to another, they had to unbutton their jackets and loosen their collars. If it had not been too awkward to carry them, Parrado would have taken off his two thick jackets, but he had to have both arms free for climbing.

"Either we freeze or burn," he muttered, wiping the sweat from his thick-lensed glasses. "And I think freezing is more comfortable."

"I don't mind the heat so much, but all this going up and down is beginning to bore me. Up one side of a mountain and down the other—up and down, up and down. It's like a damned roller coaster; and with all this snow, the peaks all look alike."

But when they reached the crest of the peak they were climbing, Parrado and Canessa happily realized they were *not* all alike, that the mountains on the next range below them were different—they had trees, thousands of pine and spruce rising straight up from the steep-angled slopes.

---

* It was subsequently learned that a team of geologists had made the cross, presumably for aerial photographs that were part of a survey.

"Ole! Ole!" yelled Canessa, throwing his arms around Parrado. "We've finally arrived."

"Macanudo, viejo, macanudo!" exclaimed Parrado. "But it's still a long way."

Rapidly descending the slope, for there was much less snow on the western side, they settled for the night on a narrow, flat rock near the base. The snow around them was not very deep, but it had a crackly crust and an icy sheen indicating partial daytime melting and freezing temperatures at night. So once again they huddled close to each other and took alternate shifts on the night watch. Elated by the prospect of touching something green after two months of nothing but snow and rock, Parrado found no difficulty staying awake. But when it was his turn to sleep, the accumulated fatigue of six days' steady climbing was like a triple dose of morphine.

On the morning of the seventh day, less than a mile from where they had slept, they came across the head of a river later identified as the Rio Carillo. Around it they could see a web of tiny flat streams seeping down the western slope of the mountain where the snows were rapidly thawing, feeding into a wide gap that got narrower and deeper as it changed from a mere creek to a full-fledged river.

"We'll follow it down," said Parrado, dipping his hand into the cold crystalline water and splashing his face with it. "Unless it gets away from us."

"How could that happen?"

"Well, it might slice through a narrow canyon that has sheer cliffs on both sides—with no space for us to pass. Then we'll have to circle around and catch the river further down."

Two hours later, they reached a chasm where the river merged with two lesser streams from the southern slope of an adjoining mountain, creating a much stronger current that flowed over a rocky precipice and tumbled roaringly into a steep canyon.

"A waterfall!" shouted Canessa against the deafening

roar of the cascading water. "It must be at least three hundred feet high."

"Beautiful," said Parrado, making no effort to be heard. "My god, how beautiful!" Then, with a deep sigh, "But we've got some problems, Roberto. That's a long way down, and there's no elevator."

The next forty-five minutes were the most terrifying and exhausting of their entire journey. After probing the topmost boulder for a secure niche in which to clamp their hooks, they lowered their climbing straps into a void just above a narrow ledge; then, with a whispered prayer, they worked their way around the pot-bellied rock, their arms strained to the limit when their shoes kept slipping off the slick surface of the stone. Gasping for breath and dizzy from exertion, they finally managed to get past that first obstacle. The waterfall thundering in his ears so that it was impossible to talk, Parrado looked down the steep gorge and watched the falling water battering against two huge rocks at the very bottom, erratic gushers of spray and foam partially obscuring the surrounding area. Looking away to avoid the hypnotic pull of the down-rushing water, he closed his eyes for a while before proceeding to the next ledge, which lay at an oblique angle. It was less difficult to reach than the first one, but it was covered with a slimy moss that was dangerously slippery.

"This is a hell of a lot worse than climbing that damned volcano," mumbled Canessa, "no matter how icy it was."

"I'm afraid so," Parrado admitted, arching his back to relieve the pulsating pain in his waist and shoulders. "But we're committed now—we can't possibly go back."

With the sun beating down on him, Parrado gradually lowered himself toward a flat rock that jutted from the concave wall of the canyon some twelve or thirteen feet below him, his feet dangling in the air like a puppet on strings. He would have to swing himself inward to reach it, and he prayed the hook would hold onto the

ledge above and that his knotted-together climbing
straps would not snap from the added strain. (How
ironic it would be to get killed on this final lap after
having survived the misery of sixty days in the frozen
cordillera!) Mumbling a one-sentence prayer, he swung
toward the rock and landed safely, both knees buckling
in the aftermath of fear. Then, with his throat still dry
and constricted, he watched Canessa come down inch
by inch, his dangling feet toe-probing in a void until
Parrado reached out and helped him in.

"Never again," said Canessa as he flopped onto the
rock. "I never, never want to do that again. I've just
shaved ten years off my life, Fernando. And with all
the other years I've lost these past seven days, I don't
have any left."

"I guess we're like cats," said Parrado. "We have
many more lives to live."

The rest of the way down was less treacherous but
still exhausting, so they allowed themselves a half hour
rest at the bottom, lying on their backs and staring in
wonder at the roaring waterfall. Refreshed in spirit if
not completely recuperated, they continued hiking along
the edge of the river all afternoon, walking through
clusters of pine trees, inhaling the pungent aroma of
evergreen. Contrasted with the cold, astringent, almost
odorless atmosphere of the high Andes, the heavily-
scented air at this lower altitude seemed to clog their
nostrils at first, but they soon got used to it. The com-
mingled scents of pine and spruce seemed even stronger, more penetrating, when they pitched camp after
sundown near the river bank.

"I've got aches in every bone and every muscle,"
Parrado said. "It's a damned wonder I can still move,
I'm so tired."

"That's exactly how I feel," said Canessa. "I thought
my body would quit on me when we were coming down
that canyon by the waterfall."

Surely they would have empathized with Saint-Exupery's protagonist, Guillaumet, who had also dragged
himself through the high sierras (but for a much

shorter period), thereafter explaining his physical reaction as follows:

"The body, then, is no more than a good instrument, no more than a servant. And on certain occasions one takes great pride in a good instrument. Thus, after I'd had nothing to eat for three days, you can imagine how my heart is ready to give up. Well, finally, as I am crawling up a vertical precipice that hangs over a void, probing blindly for something to hold onto, my heart stops. It vacillates a moment, then starts beating again, but loses rhythm. I'm sure if it vacillates one second more, I'll surely die. Without moving a muscle, I listen to myself. Never, I tell you, never have I felt so close to my heart. I tell it, 'Come on, one more time—try to beat again.' And because it's a heart of fine quality, it vacillates only an instant, then starts beating again. If you could only imagine how proud of my heart I was!"

Neither Parrado nor Canessa would have any trouble understanding such pride in one's heart—or one's entire body, for that matter. Theirs had certainly served them well in the most terrifying crises. So, on that seventh night they gave their bodies a longer rest than usual, confident their journey would soon end, that they would find help for their companions in a day or so.

But on the following day their luck turned sour. As they were crossing the river to get to the side that had fewer obstacles, Canessa slipped on one of the stepping stones and splashed into the water, banging one leg on a sharp rock. Dragging himself out of the swift rapids with Parrado's help, he managed to struggle to the opposite shore and crawled onto a low bank.

"I'll be okay in a few minutes," he said. "It's just a bump, Fernando."

But a swelling immediately developed and he was suffering acute pain. As a third-year medical student, he knew instantly that he should put no pressure on the leg and should probably remain immobile for several days. Nevertheless, he tried to get up after a brief rest, but had to lie down again before he could take a second step.

Fernando Parrado, after seventy days in the high Andes. With Roberto Canessa, he brought the first word of their incredible survival, and led the rescue helicopters back over the mountains to bring out the remaining survivors.
(Alvaro Covacevich, EMELCO films)

The snowbound peaks of the Andes, similar to the site where the Uruguayan rugby team's plane went down.
(BLACK STAR)

Sergio Catalan Martinez, the cattleman who found Canessa and Parrado after their exhausting ten-day journey in search of help. (EMELCO)

A fragment of the note written by Parrado. Wrapping it around a rock, he threw it across the river to Martinez, who rode to the military outpost at Puente Negro to recount the dramatic survival story. (EMELCO)

Parrado and Canessa on horseback on the first leg of their journey to the hospital at Santiago.   (EMELCO)

Canessa speaks with members of the Andean Rescue
Corps, led by Commander Morell of the Chilean Army.
(EMELCO)

Pointing to a map, Canessa shows the
newspapermen the location of the plane
and survivors.   (EMELCO)

Survivors of the crash rejoice as they embrace the rescue team after they were brought down by helicopters to San Fernando.   (EMELCO)

A helicopter brings the first rescue team to the scene of the crash.   (Alvaro Covacevich, EMELCO)

Near starvation after seventy days on the mountainside, several of the fourteen remaining survivors gather by the fuselage of the wrecked plane in this photo taken from the rescue helicopter. (UPI)

The nosewheel and smashed cockpit of the plane show the force of impact. (EMELCO)

Jubilant survivors welcome the rescuers, heedless of the ghastly debris with which they have lived for weeks. Note human leg in foreground. (EMELCO)

Above: The remains of some of the victims lie in rubble near the hulk of the shattered Uruguayan Air Force plane.

Below: Two more of the bodies. Many of the twenty-nine who died were later consumed by the sixteen survivors.
(WIDE WORLD PHOTOS)

The last eight survivors huddle in the craft's fuselage on their final night before rescue. Still rejoicing at their miraculous rescue, they are unprepared for the sensation their story will make in the world news media.

(WIDE WORLD PHOTOS)

A human foot and partially eaten leg rest beside the nose-wheel. No attempt had been made to conceal these hor-rifying sights from the rescuers. (WIDE WORLD PHOTOS)

On their return from the crash site by helicopter, survivors
are rushed to the hospital in Santiago.   (EMELCO)

Fernando Parrado with his father. Already there are un-
asked questions. . . .   (EMELCO)

Roy Harley is greeted by his mother. (WIDE WORLD PHOTOS)

Eduardo Strauch with his sweetheart. (EMELCO)

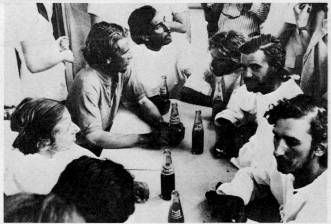

At the hospital in Santiago, survivors sip soft drinks and talk to the staff. They have been advised to be silent about what is past. (WIDE WORLD PHOTOS)

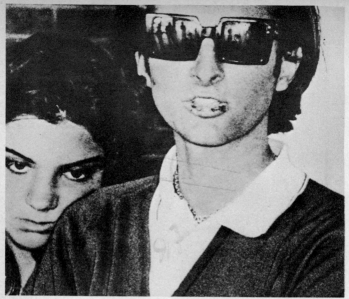

Arrival at the airport in Montevideo, Uruguay. (EMELCO)

Before departure, survivors attend a Mass of Thanksgiving at a church in San Fernando, at the foot of the mountains. (EMELCO)

High on the mountain, at the site of the crash, members of the Andean Rescue Corps attend a burial service for those who died.   (EMELCO)

A Roman Catholic priest says a funeral mass over the common grave of the twenty-nine victims who died in the crash and in the long weeks before rescue came.

(WIDE WORLD PHOTOS)

"You'd better go on," he said to Fernando. "We're almost there."

"No, Roberto, I can't leave you here alone."

"But you must, Fernando. You've got to go on without me. Time is running short."

"I can't and I won't leave you alone."

"Don't worry about me, *che!* I'll be all right, I tell you. You'll be back for me in a couple of days."

But Parrado, who logically feared an attack by wildcats or wolves, was adamant. "Listen, Roberto, we started together and we'll damned well finish together. Even if we have to die together, *che,* I'm not going to abandon you."

Hoping that a few hours' rest would improve Canessa's condition, they "took a vacation" for the remainder of the day, Parrado meanwhile exploring the surrounding area to determine the most feasible route for the next day's journey. Since he had decided to carry Canessa on his shoulders in modified piggyback fashion or to convert himself into a human crutch, Parrado had to look for the most level ground, even though it might not be the shortest way.

"We'll cut through those pine trees and then cross through a valley on the other side," he suggested. "The river route's a little rocky up ahead."

On the following morning, as they passed through a shady grove of pine and spruce, they noticed several hoof prints and clusters of horse manure not far from the embers of a campfire. Then, an hour later, they came across the first animals they had seen in ten weeks—about twenty cows peacefully grazing in the lower part of a narrow valley.

"Look at those cows," yelled Canessa, nearly falling off Parrado's back. "There's a whole herd!"

"They could be wild bulls," cautioned Parrado, staring nearsightedly through his homemade sunglasses. "We'd better be careful."

"No, no, Fernando! They're really cows. Take off those goggles and put on your regular glasses. You can see their tits, for God's sake!"

Easing Canessa to the ground, then quickly replacing the goggles with his horn-rimmed glasses, Parrado took a second look and grinned. "Beautiful," he said in soft-voiced wonder. "They're absolutely beautiful. We're finally back to civilization."

But there were no ranchers in sight, nor any horses. And after an hour's search in several directions, Parrado concluded there were no ranches or any kind of habitation within walking distance. "These may be wild cows," he said on his return. "Just wandering around the mountains."

"They can't be," insisted Canessa, looking once more at the docile herd. "They're domesticated, *che*. Some-one owns them, I'm sure; and he's bound to come around soon."

"Not necessarily, Roberto. He might not come around for another week or two. They probably don't need much tending. Just feed themselves from one place to another. So I don't think we can wait for the owner to come around. We've got fourteen friends back there, and we've already been gone nine days."

"Then you'd better go on by yourself tomorrow," said Canessa. "We must be pretty close to a village, or at least a ranch. And I'll be safe here—with those cows to protect me."

"Maybe you're right," Parrado agreed. "We've got rivers on both sides now, and they converge about a mile from here. So we're caught in a wedge, a sort of *cul de sac*. But I still don't want to leave you."

"There's no danger, Fernando. I'll be okay. I've still got some rations and plenty of fresh water."

Parrado nodded, then frowned as if a difficult prob-lem had crossed his mind.

"Well, maybe I'd better kill one of those cows, and cook some meat for you. Plenty of wood here, and I've got my cigarette lighter."

Canessa grinned and leaned back on his right elbow. "And how will you kill it? With your bare hands?"

Pursing his lips as he turned to look at the still mo-tionless herd, a frown of deep concentration creasing his brow, Parrado finally said, "That won't be too hard, Roberto. First of all, I'll shove one of them under a tree. Then I'll climb on a limb right above it and drop a big rock on its head. *Whop!* Just like that."

Doubled over with laughter and gasping for breath, Canessa temporarily forgot the pain that had immobilized him. "For a moment there, I had pictured Manolete coming over the horns for a graceful kill," he said when he had caught his breath. "But you suddenly changed him into a Charlie Chaplin. With a *whop!* Instead of an *Ole.*"

Asserting that a "hungry cowfighter" has no time for art, Parrado desisted from killing a cow that evening. But he did build a lively campfire with dry twigs and broken tree branches apparently strewn about by heavy winds. Later, just before their evening prayers, they ate double portions of the meat they had brought along, both of them realizing the remaining supply would spoil quickly in the warmer region they had now reached. Briefly contemplating that possibility, Parrado went on to a more disturbing speculation about a problem they would soon be facing: *How would they explain their consumption of human flesh?* Most Chileans knew there was no source of food in the high Andes—no plants, no animals, no birds, no fish. And Canessa had told him that any doctor would know they could survive only by eating human flesh, the only possible source of proteins for anyone stranded at such altitudes. So there was no way of concealing what they had done. How, then, should they answer the questions that were sure to be asked? And what would they say to the families of those whose bodies had been eaten?

Having convinced themselves that they had done nothing wrong, that they had had no other choice, the survivors nevertheless feared outsiders might not understand. Some might, indeed, disapprove, though refraining from outright condemnation. Consequently, they spent hours theorizing about the problem, ultimately concluding they would have to "play it by ear."

"There's no way of knowing how people will react,"

Paez had said. "We'll just have to roll with the punches, as my father always says."

Recalling the arguments and counterarguments applying to this or that approach, Parrado eventually dozed off and enjoyed the best night's sleep he'd had in ten weeks. Refreshed and anxious to get moving again, he was up at sunrise, and a half hour later he was carrying Canessa on his back and headed west toward the merger of the two rivers. Around ten o'clock, Canessa suddenly spied two horsemen about three hundred meters beyond the river on their right.

"Look over there!" he shouted. "Some ranchers, Fernando! Let me down and go call them. Hurry, *che!*"

Easing him to the ground, Parrado galloped off toward the river, waving and shouting as he ran. But the horsemen, now riding away from the river, apparently never saw him.

"Damn it! I missed them," he told Canessa on his return. "I would have run after them, but that river looks awfully rough. I'm not sure I can make it in my condition. And it's damned noisy, by the way. They couldn't have heard me with all that roaring."

"They're bound to come back, Fernando. Or some-one else will come."

True to expectations, a lone cattleman appeared late in the afternoon. Catching his attention as he ran toward the river, Parrado nearly stumbled as he got to the edge of the water. "Can you help us!" he yelled. "We're the Uruguayans who got lost in the air crash."

Leaning forward with a hand cupped over his right ear, the horseman tried to hear, but the river was too noisy.

"Uruguayos!" yelled Parrado, his throat aching with the effort. *"Accidente! Accidente!"*

But the man still couldn't hear him. Waving and hollering as loud as he could, Parrado kept shouting, "Help! We need help!" for three or four minutes without any visible success. In his weakened state, his voice was undoubtedly much less audible than usual.

Finally, the cattleman cupped both hands around his mouth and shouted two words, *"Huelvo manana!"* (I'll come back tomorrow.)

Puzzled and disappointed, Parrado logically assumed the man was being super-cautious, if not downright apprehensive. With his dirty beard, shaggy hair, gaunt face, ragged clothing, and feverish look, Parrado knew he could easily be mistaken for a wandering hippie or a mad hermit. Cursing their luck, he and Canessa finally managed to fall asleep, suddenly jerking awake when a cow mooed in the nearby grazing area, then dozing off again.

At sunrise, Parrado was already awake, dousing his face in the cold river and trying to smooth down his straggly beard and long hair, hopefully attenuating the hippie appearance. Then he prowled the left bank of the river, debating whether to take a chance crossing it, but realizing it would be too risky. Finally, the cattleman returned. Dismounting and walking to the edge of the opposite shore, he picked up a rock, tied a piece of paper around it, and tossed it across the river. Retrieving the rock, Parrado carefully untied the piece of paper, saw that it was blank, and instantly became aware that he was expected to write a message. Fumbling through his pockets as if to search for a pen, he finally motioned that he had nothing to write with. So the cattleman wrapped a pencil stub in his handkerchief, weighting it with a stone, and threw it across the roaring water. Steadying his trembling hand, Parrado wrote out the following message:

I've come from a plane that crashed in the mountains. I'm Uruguayan. We've been traveling ten days. I have an injured friend up there. There are fourteen injured persons in the wrecked plane. We've got to get out of here rapidly, and we don't know how. We have no food. We're weak. When can you rescue us? Please. We can't travel anymore. Where are we?

The stony-faced cattleman, soon identified as Sergio Catalan Martinez, read the note with a puzzled frown, not quite believing that anyone could have survived a crash in the cordillera. So he read it again, slowly nodding his head at the end of each phrase. Then his face lit up with a smile, and he waved back excitedly.

"Huelvo pronto!" he yelled, galloping off at break-neck speed. A normally reticent man with a leathery face and crinkly eyes, the forty-four-year-old *arriero* was not given to spontaneous reactions, but he was shaken by Parrado's plea for help. But how could they have survived?

The question was still buzzing inside his brain when he reached the soldiers at a small military outpost at Puente Negro, about forty-five miles away from where he had found Parrado. Having shown them the note and urged them to send a rescue team, he hurried back to tell Parrado that help was on the way. Meanwhile, some of his friends and neighbors—Juanito Farfan, Enrique Gonzalez and Armando Cerda—had crossed the perilous river on horseback and had taken Parrado and Canessa to a small ranchhouse in a beautiful near-by valley called Los Maitenes. There they were given their first full meal in seventy-two days—several slices of goat cheese, barbecued goat, a jug of fresh milk and hot corn tortillas.

"This is food for the gods," said Canessa, between bites. "I've never eaten a better meal!"

"You've lost a lot of weight," observed Catalan, who had just joined them.

"We certainly have," said Parrado, touching his bony ribs through two tattered and soiled shirts. "I'll bet I've lost forty or fifty pounds."

"Sure looks that way," said Catalan. "What did you eat to stay alive at the altitude?"

Parrado and Canessa glanced at each other, as if to signal that they had come to what bullfighters call the "moment of truth." "Well, first of all," said Canessa, "we found a root between the rocks that made a good beverage, something you Chileans call *te de burro* (donkey tea)."

"That's right," said Farfan. "We call it that because only a jackass would like it."

"We also dug under the snow and found some small plants that produce a juice that's like cacao, but more

An X marks the spot near Alto de los Arrieros where the crash survivors endured the seventy-two-day ordeal before they were finally rescued. The arrow and broken line follow the incredible ten-day trek of Canessa and Parrado across El Tinguiririca to an area close to Los Maitenes, where they were found by a cattleman and brought to the hospital at San Fernando.

bitter. And we found some berries on shrubs that some-how poked through the snow."

"And we caught some birds and a few fish now and then—from the lake at the base of the mountain," Par-rado added. "We also had lots of cheese, chocolate, and wine that we'd bought in Mendoza."

"You were lucky to find anything," said Catalan, smiling. "God was with you. He wanted you to live."

The rescue squad arrived at the ranch in Los Mai-tenes at ten o'clock that night, and when they started asking the anticipated questions about what the survi-vors had fed on, Catalan and Farfan excitedly broke in with the information they had previously heard from Parrado and Canessa.

"We're awfully tired," said Parrado, not wanting to hear any more discussion about food. "And we'll have to get up early for the helicopter you mentioned ear-lier."

"Yes, we certainly will. They're sending two helicop-ters as early as possible, Fernando."

"Great. I'm anxious to see the fourteen people we left behind."

He did not know that a small army of reporters were on their way to Los Maitenes by jeep and horseback, that millions of people had already learned that two survivors of the crash had been found. The reporters would descend upon them shortly after sunrise, and their questions were likely to be more insistent than those of the less inquistive ranch hands, who had treated them like long-lost sons.

VI

Secrecy and Guilt

The local mountain police had been highly skeptical when Sergio Catalan told them about Parrado and showed them the note he had written. They couldn't believe anyone could possibly survive for some seventy days in the barren heights of the cordillera.

"It might be a hoax by a couple of hippies," one of them said, glancing at the scrawled message. "They're always pulling queer stunts."

"But this man was nearly starved to death," Catalan insisted. "And his friend was too sick to walk anymore. They're not really hippies, *mi capitan*—they just look that way because they haven't shaved or taken a bath for two months."

Though still dubious, the *carabineros'* suspicions lessened a bit when Juan Farfan produced a ballpoint pen which Canessa had given him. "Look at this lettering on the side," he said, pointing to the trademark. "It was manufactured in Uruguay, so you know he's really an Uruguayan."

"Well, anyone could have a pen like that, Sergio. But I guess it could be true. Miracles do happen."

Some reporters were equally dubious when the news was relayed to Santiago later that afternoon. One well-known news broadcaster immediately went on the air and flatly declared that the report was a "clever lie" by President Salvador Allende's administration "to detract public attention from the miserable economic mess that he's got us into." Most of the media, however, accepted the report at face value and flashed the news all over the world. Meanwhile, a swarm of correspondents commandeered every available taxi cab and rushed to the town of San Fernando, where the Air Force helicopters would reportedly bring the sixteen survivors. When informed that rescue operations had been delayed till the following day, thirty or forty reporters hired jeeps and horses for an all-night trip to Los Maitenes, hoping to interview and photograph Parrado and Canessa near the very spot where they had first been seen by Catalan.

Huddled together in the back seat of the pace-setting jeep, three of the European contingent kept one another awake speculating about various techniques for survival in the high Andes. How could you avoid freezing to death? How could anyone survive a plane crash where there was no possible place for an emergency landing? Why had the plane so completely disappeared from sight? Were any of the survivors seriously injured —and, if so, what kind of medical attention could they have received? But the most insistent question was a question almost classic in its stark simplicity: What had they eaten to avoid starving to death?

Their fellow reporters in Santiago had said there were no plants, no animals, no birds, nothing at all at that altitude except rock and snow. And although a plane on a two-hour flight might carry a few tidbits, it was unlikely to carry enough food to feed sixteen persons for seventy-two days.

How, then, could they possibly have survived?

With that question (and many more, of course) poised on the tips of their collective tongues, the reporters finally got to the ranch cabin at Los Maitenes just after sunrise. But Parrado and Canessa were still asleep—and they were not to be disturbed by anyone, "not even by the President himself," Catalan firmly announced.

Finally, at 10:00 A.M., the two instant celebrities emerged from the cabin and were immediately surrounded by a jackal-pack of writers and cameramen, each hungering for his morsel of news, pushing and elbowing each other to get a closer look. But the uni-

formed *militia* quickly interceded, telling the reporters
that the two men would answer only a few questions.

"There isn't much time right now," their captain
explained. "We've got to take them over to the helicopters, so they can direct the pilots to where their friends
are. We've got to hurry, *senores*. Perhaps they'll hold a
press conference when they get to San Fernando—at
the hospital."

But Parrado and Canessa did answer a few preliminary questions: "We're feeling fine. . . . It took us
ten days to get down here. . . . There were sixteen men
who survived. . . . All the others were killed instantly
or died afterward in a huge avalanche. . . . Yes, we'll
be happy to get back to Montevideo. . . ." But neither
the questions nor the answers were very specific. And
if anyone asked the question that was paramount in
everyone's mind, it was apparently drowned out by all
the lesser inquiries, or was simply ignored by Parrado
and Canessa as they were led toward some horses.

Just before mounting the second horse, Parrado
noticed a female reporter with a pained, sorrowful expression on her face. "What's wrong, *senorita?*" he
asked with gentle concern. "You seem so sad."

"It's nothing," said Manola Robles. "Just my ankle
—hurting a little. I sprained it last night riding in a
jeep."

Parrado smiled sympathetically. "Don't let it bother
you. We've also been through a few bad moments; but,
as you can see, we're still alive. So why don't you
smile a little, *senorita?* You'll feel better."

Looking at the twenty-three-year-old survivor as if
he were a wise old man, Ms. Robles allowed a slow
smile to spread across her lovely face, yet her dark
brown eyes reflected a profound sorrow, as if she were
privy to the unimaginable tragedies suffered by Parrado. As a woman reporter, with a special aptitude for
significant details, perhaps she had particularly noticed
that there were only *male* survivors and that among the
female passengers there had been two named Parrado
—Fernando's mother and sister. Yet, with all his own

personal sorrow, he had reached out to comfort her, a total stranger.

Again smiling in her direction, his brown eyes diminished in size by thick concave lenses that indicated lifelong myopia, Parrado mounted his horse in one easy motion, sitting in tandem behind an already mounted soldier. With a Chilean news broadcaster jogging alongside them, adjusting his bulky portable transmitter and poking a microphone in Parrado's face, they rode to a broad meadow where the helicopters were waiting. Still trailing them as they boarded the ten-passenger aircraft, the panting, sweaty-faced reporter yelled the question he'd been wanting to ask all along: "And what did you eat to stay alive?"

"We'll talk about those things later on," Parrado answered. "We've got to find our friends first."

When Parrado and Canessa boarded the helicopter, some of the reporters rushed to their jeeps and horses for an immediate return to San Fernando, hoping to get back in time for the promised press conference at the hospital. Others remained at Los Maitenes to watch the takeoff; and when Flight Commander Carlos Garcia told everyone there would be a delay of one or two hours because of poor weather conditions, three foreign correspondents once again approached Parrado, who seemed more physically recuperated than Canessa.

"Fernando," said one who spoke with an Argentine accent, "there seems to be a rather incredible situation here. You remained in the very heights of the cordillera, covered with snow for more than two months. There's no doubt that the very meagre food supplies on the plane were soon exhausted, no matter how carefully you rationed them. That's why we ask how you managed to survive without starving to death, or at least going insane with hunger."

Darting a quick side-glance at Canessa, Parrado quietly but firmly avoided a direct answer. "We ate the food stored in the airplane and also the food we had purchased in Mendoza. After that—well, we just survived. But there are certain things we will never talk about, things that make no sense now and which are not worth remembering. And what I tell you is what we all feel. No, no—we're not going to talk about them."

But Roberto Canessa had already concluded it would be impossible to hide the truth. As a medical student, he knew that any doctor would quickly guess how they had avoided starvation. So would any intelligent journalist. Consequently, about a half hour later (after he had conferred with Parrado), he confided everything to one of the two doctors who were to accompany them on the rescue mission, Dr. Eduardo Arriagada, the youthful but experienced director of medical services for the regional military base at San Fernando. Recalling in grim detail the first few days following the avalanche, when everyone was on the verge of starvation, Canessa gave the doctor an almost verbatim account of their final conversation with Dr. Nicola.

"Realizing he himself would soon be dead because of his very serious injuries, Dr. Nicola told us we would eventually die (and probably go insane before dying) unless we could provide ourselves with proteins. And that's when he advised us to eat the flesh of our dead companions, since their bodies were the only possible protein source. I had already known that, of course, but I just couldn't face it. But he begged us to do it—and to convince the others, telling us he would be proud to sacrifice his own flesh to save someone else."

Nodding his head like an understanding priest or parent, Dr. Arriagada could see that Canessa and Parrado were greatly relieved to have the truth surface. "Dr. Nicola was entirely right," he said when they had finished their "confession." "You had no other course, my friends. Any one of us would do exactly the same as you did. There was no point in dying needlessly. And no real harm was done to anyone. Your friends were already dead, their souls long gone to another world. But I don't think you should discuss this matter with the press, or with anyone else. Some things are better left unsaid. And I solemnly promise not to say a word of this to anyone."

Having first been assured they had done no wrong, Parrado and Canessa must have wondered why Dr. Arriagada was (in the next breath) telling them not to talk about it—as if it were something to be ashamed of.

Clearly baffled by such contradictory and unsettling advice, Parrado merely nodded and said, "Thank you, Doctor. We appreciate your listening to us."

"Parrado seemed somewhat distracted after our discussions," the doctor later told a colleague, apparently unaware of the ambiguous impression he himself had made. "He must have been wrestling with some internal dilemma—trying to come to terms with himself. But he quickly snapped out of his mood when we finally took off at noon."

Unfortunately, the weather had not improved during the two-hour wait. The winds were fierce and erratic, the heavy gray clouds thicker than before.

"That's an awfully low ceiling," said Commander Garcia, maneuvering the first helicopter between a pair of towering pine trees. "And this damned fog will certainly raise hell with our visibility. So I guess we'll have to follow the river as far as we can."

There were six men sitting behind the pilot—Parrado, Dr. Arriagada, an army medical corporal named Jose Bravo Castro, and three members of the famed Andean Rescue Corps—Claudio Lucero, Sergio Diaz, and Osvaldo Villegas. Though outwardly unworried when the helicopter bounced and jostled against treacherous crosswinds, they were intensely quiet as Commander Garcia snaked his way along the shifting course of the Rio Tinguiririca, occasionally leaning toward the windows to get a better view of the rock-battering rapids and cataracts. When they suddenly came upon a thundering waterfall which forced the somewhat surprised pilot to lift the helicopter at a desperately steep angle, Parrado recognized the rocky abutments on either side, particularly the high, slippery ledge where he and Canessa had felt hopelessly stranded.

"We came down this way," Parrado told Arriagada as they fluttered past it. "And it got pretty rough at this point."

"Do helicopters always bounce like this?" asked Parnando."

Just beyond the waterfall were heavy, low-lying patches of fog that forced the pilot to fly even lower than before, twenty or thirty feet above the thrashing river. The helicopter shook and lurched as it squeezed through a narrow canyon.

"Do helicopters always bounce like this?" asked Parrado, during a brief respite.

"Not always," said the pilot. "These winds are pretty bitchy today. And I'm afraid it'll get much worse up ahead."

It was, in fact, far worse than the pilot had anticipated. Five minutes later, when they had got past the riverhead and were cruising at an altitude of a thousand feet between two snow-covered peaks, they were caught in a wicked downdraft that drove them into a near tailspin. Dropping over nine hundred feet in less than thirty seconds, they gritted their teeth and prepared for a violent crash, one of the passengers yelling, *"No! No! No!"* But at the very last moment, the pilot managed to regain control and made the helicopter swoop into a horizontal glide, skimming across a narrow valley like a giant albatross.

"That was a close one," said Parrado, drawing a deep breath. "I was sure we'd be killed."

"Now, that would be real irony," said the pilot, expertly swerving through a narrow gap. "For you to get killed at the very end—after all you've been through—that would be one goddamned shame. But, by God, I won't let it happen, Fernando!"

"I trust you," said Parrado. "You're a damned good pilot!"

"Also lucky, my friend. You need lots of luck in this cordillera—especially with these damned air currents coming from—"

His voice broke off as the aircraft hit another air

pocket, floundering and jerking like a crippled hawk, then suddenly smoothing out less than twenty feet from the base of the mountain.

"That was a real bitch!" the pilot yelled, hunching forward like a bronco buster.

But once again the helicopter quaked and bounced and finally zoomed away safely before touching the frozen slope, leaning with a stiff wind as it glided around the next slope. Looking back, Parrado could see the second helicopter following them at a slightly higher level, and he imagined Canessa crouching next to the pilot and wondering how they had ever got through these godforsaken mountains.

"Recognize this area?" the pilot asked Parrado. "We're getting pretty high now."

"Can't be sure," he said, straining his eyes. "The damned clouds are so thick and low, you can't see the summit. But that one—the one straight ahead—looks like the base of the volcano I told you about. I can't see the top, but the bottom looks familiar."

"That's El Tinguiririca," said the pilot. "One of the highest in all the Andes, *amigo.*"

"Well, that's the one, I think. I remember that gorge near the base."

"You climbed that?" asked one of the veteran alpinists of the Rescue Corps, who was leaning over the pilot's shoulder. "You climbed to the very top?"

"We had to," said Parrado. "We had to get an overall view of where we were going."

"My God!" exclaimed another alpinist. "Very few people have ever climbed that volcano—very few."

"But we'll go around the bottom," said the pilot, swinging the helicopter into a low arc. "It's much safer this way."

Not entirely safe, however. A stiff wind caught them as they cleared the northern slope and came over the snow-covered lake, the surrounding peaks almost totally obscured by a dense soupy fog.

"We're over there," said Parrado, pointing at an angle. "On a high ledge."

"Don't see anything," said the pilot.

"You'll have to go higher."

The helicopter wobbled through swirling winds, gradually reaching an altitude of fifteen hundred feet above the lake, where the fog yielded only minimal visibility.

"Over this way now," said Parrado, as he looked for a familiar landmark. "It should be somewhere around here. But you'll have to dip through this fog, I guess."

"Okay. Here goes."

Descending slowly through the fog cloud, probing tentatively like a blind cat in a strange room, the helicopter dipped lower and lower, wobbling and jouncing in renewed turbulence, instantly reminding Parrado of the F-27 diving blindly through the same kind of cloud cover just before the crash. Then, as he sucked in his breath and braced himself for another crash, the helicopter finally poked through the vaporous underbelly of the fog, and Parrado spotted the crippled fuselage 150 feet away.

"There it is!" he shouted, his temples suddenly throbbing. "There it is—there it is! Oh my God! We've finally found them!"

But as Commander Garcia began his approach, gently easing the helicopter down to the ledge as if it were a fat old lady about to sit down on a fragile chair, a violent wind caught them broadside and shook them off course. Cursing angrily, and swerving to accommodate another crosswind, Garcia regained his course and gradually dipped toward the snow-covered ledge.

The fourteen wildly excited survivors came into clear focus as the helicopter drew closer, but the pilot suddenly noticed a new threat. "I'm afraid we can't land," he said, narrowing his eyes into a dark scowl. "That snow's fairly deep, and there's probably a hard crust on top."

"You're right," said Parrado. "It's almost like ice. It cracks under your feet."

"God damn it—I should have known that!" the pilot said. "We've got a real problem, Fernando."

"But why?"

"Because if I land on that surface, I won't be able to take off again. My landing skis will get stuck. Jesus Christ and Mary—what a mess!"

They were now hovering over the survivors, most of them waving and shouting like children at a picnic— Parrado waving back but wondering if they could possibly be rescued by helicopter (with a rope ladder perhaps?) or if they would have to travel by land, climbing and hiking for several days. Which might be impossible for some of them.

"I've got a solution," said the pilot. "Let's hope it works."

"What's the plan?" asked Dr. Arriagada, leaning over his shoulder.

"Well, first of all, I'm going to lower this copter so that it's barely off the ground—ten or twelve inches, maybe. Then I want the three mountain climbers and the medical attendant to hop off and ask six men to come aboard—those who are most severely disabled. Then, while I'm taking that bunch back to Los Maitenes, you four men can clear away the snow for a landing pad on my return. Meanwhile, I'm going to tell the other helicopter to go back. Too big a risk for both of us."

Grinning happily and impulsively patting the doctor's shoulder, Parrado leaned toward the window and waved again as the pilot carefully lowered the craft and tilted it so that one ski barely touched the snow while the other remained aloft. Minutes later, the helicopter zoomed into the air again, carrying six new passengers: Carlos Paez, Jr., Eduardo Strauch, Ramon Sabella, Antonio Vicintin, Daniel Fernandez, and Alvaro Mangino. Hugging each one as he came aboard, Parrado had seen the eight other survivors warmly embracing the three alpinists and Cpl. Bravo.

Twenty minutes later, after what Mangino called a "crazy roller coaster ride" through windswept valleys and narrow canyons, the helicopter landed at Los Maitenes, where the passengers and crew rested a while before proceeding to the hospital in San Fernando, where an army of reporters, friends, relatives, and local residents were preparing a triumphant welcome for them.

Meanwhile, the four outsiders who had stayed with the other eight survivors were about to witness something they never would have imagined—not even in the most horrifying nightmare.

Having greeted the four members of the rescue team as if they were long-lost brothers, nearly smothering them with warm embraces, the eight left-behind survivors led them toward what one of them called "our grand hotel." Words and phrases tumbled over each other, one question ricocheting off another, as everyone tried to talk at once. But their spirited conversation abruptly sputtered to an awkward silence when one of the alpinists, Claudio Lucero, suddenly stepped on a mutilated hand half-buried in the snow. Shrinking back as if it were a snake, Lucero stared in shock and disbelief, a cold chill racing down his spine as he noticed that most of the flesh was missing from the palm. Then he saw the bare bones of the forearm and several other disfigured limbs lying in the snow—dismembered arms and legs, fleshless torsos, and a human skull half-submerged in crusty ice.

"But you must have known!" said one of the survivors, apparently shaken by the horrified reactions of Lucero, Diaz, Villegas, and Bravo. "Someone must have told you—either Parrado or Canessa. They must have told someone. Because we had to do it. There was no other way to survive. We had—"

"Perhaps they did," said Cpl. Bravo, the medical attendant, who seemed less shocked than the three alpinists. "They may have told Dr. Arriagada. I saw them talking. But, anyway, we understand. We know you had to do it. There was no other choice."

"But no one told *you*. That's why you're so horrified," said the man who had spoken first. "They should have told you! So you'd be prepared for this."

"It must be awful for you," said another survivor,

glancing at the human remains strewn about the fuselage. "And I guess we've got too used to it, too blase
—but we couldn't have stood it otherwise."

Determined to regain his poise, Lucero put his arm
around the youth nearest him. "We understand," he
said, speaking slowly, as if searching for the most appropriate words. "These things happen, you know. I
mean we've all got to make tough decisions now and
then—no matter what other people think. Especially
when your life is at stake, and—well, when there's no
other way, I guess you've got to do what has to be
done. And people will have to understand—and try to
put themselves in your shoes."

"Then you do understand?"

"Well. . . . Like I said before—I mean, I guess
most people would understand—even if they're pretty
shocked at first—that you did what you had to do."

Sensing that Lucero's ambivalence was painfully obvious, Cpl. Bravo interrupted in a resolute voice: "I
would do exactly the same as you did. And I would
feel no guilt about it. You had no other choice."

Nevertheless, three minutes later, Bravo himself was
stunned by the macabre spectacle inside the makeshift
dormitory. Hanging from the rafters were several strips
of human flesh, still moist with draining blood that
glowed like neon in the afternoon light.

"The smell was awful inside that fuselage," Bravo
later told Arriagada. "I wanted to vomit right then and
there. But I clamped my mouth tight and waited for the
nausea to go away."

Apparently choosing to ignore any sign of revulsion
on the part of the four rescuers—perhaps thinking they
would have to be shocked into acknowledging the harsh
realities they themselves had by necessity accepted—the
eight survivors seemed almost nonchalant about the
multilated arms, legs, and other parts of human bodies
lying outside the fuselage. ("Why haven't they buried
all this?" Bravo kept asking himself. "It would have
been so easy to conceal everything. After all, they had
heard on the radio that a rescue team was coming. So

why had they left everything out in the open?") Yet, a kind of innocence characterized their apparent nonchalance, an aura of guiltlessness that made everything seem unreal, chimeric.

"Like a strange fantasy," Bravo later described the scene.

When, for example, Lucero picked up a skull and asked who it belonged to, one of the survivors calmly told him it was the pilot's head. "We took the brain, but we didn't eat his body," he added matter-of-factly. "We couldn't get it out of the cabin. The walls had caved in and his body was trapped inside—and too stiff to move."

They went on to explain how Canessa had used razor blades to sever the flesh from the bodies. "Then we hung the pieces of meat from the ceiling of the cabin because Canessa wanted to have the fats and oils that dripped from them. He used the oils to make salves or ointments; and we rubbed the fat on our arms and legs to protect our skin against the cold and the damned winds."

"God helped us," said one of the younger survivors. "When the avalanche hit us on the sixteenth day, killing seven or eight people, we buried five of the bodies in the frozen snow; so it was like having a refrigerator to keep them from spoiling and getting putrid."

Six of the bodies had not been used—three women and three men. The remains of several other bodies were casually identified by Gustavo Zervino, a lively and friendly nineteen-year-old who apparently had no sense of guilt. "There was some resistance at first," he told Bravo as they started to clear a space for the helicopter to land on. "But Canessa and Parrado finally convinced us. Dr. Nicola had told them that we would starve to death or go crazy if we didn't have proteins. And the only possible source of proteins was human flesh. So we had to do it."

"I fully agree," said Bravo. "But I imagine some were hard to convince."

"Yes, that's true. In fact, one of my friends wanted

to kill himself. So Fernando had to hide the gun—the pilot's gun—and all the bullets. And later on, Numa Turcatti . . ."

"Well, what about Turcatti?"

"He let himself starve to death," Zervino answered, his voice suddenly husky and pensive. "He wouldn't eat the meat. He kept hiding it. And when we tried to force him—knowing he would die without it—he would spit it out. Poor Numa—he was so stubborn."

"Or maybe it was courage," said someone else. "He had the courage of his convictions."

There was an abrupt silence after he spoke, an awkward hiatus in the overlapping conversations, and a sudden concentration on the removal of snow for the landing pad. When they had cleared a space of about 150 square feet, mumbling occasional comments about the snow and the furious winds, their talk gradually became more spirited and even amusing. They joked about the "crazy, childish" arguments they had got into, and the fist fights between lifelong friends simply because one of them had failed to say "good morning" or had turned the wrong way when they were sleeping together like packed sardines.

"You can get awfully goddamned mad when someone rubs his lousy beard against your ear," remarked Javier Methol, no doubt referring to a personal incident. "Especially when you're frostbitten. But you learn to hold your temper."

"Until it happens once too often," said Zervino. "Then, wham! You've got a fight going."

"Were there many fights like that?" asked Lucero, grinning at Zervino's comic demonstration of a wild uppercut to someone's imaginary chin.

"Not many," Javier said. "Well—maybe there *were* more fights at certain times."

"When would that be?"

"Whenever things got tight. Like the first few days after we heard the search was over. We got awfully depressed when they announced it on the radio, and some of us got kinda short-tempered. Frustrated, I guess."

"I think it was worse after the avalanche," said Adolfo Strauch. "We had run short of food, and our rations were nothing really—not enough to feed a rat. And then those damned hunger pains were. . . . Well, I'd rather not talk about it. But, anyway, we had quite a few arguments. And fights, too."

"That's when Canessa and Paez had a fight," some-one recalled. "I guess it started with a stupid argument about the menu at Morini's or maybe El Aguila."

"The menu?" asked Bravo, frowning slightly. "They fought about a menu?"

"Well, it started that way, I guess. We were always arguing about restaurants and menus. Part of a game we played to pass away the time. Roberto would say that Morini's served the best snails, and Carlos would say they were lousy, and then you'd have a few insults flying around, and maybe a real fist fight."

"Since we're talking about food," said Lucero, break-ing into a long pause, "I think it's time to eat. But I don't want any arguments about the menu."

"What have you got?"

"Soup, sandwiches, and coffee."

"That's food for the gods!" They sat in small groups outside the cabin, grabbing the proffered sandwiches as if they were Christmas presents and gobbling them quickly, hoping to finish before the helicopter returned. But after three hours of patient waiting, the alpinists assumed that bad weather conditions had forced the Air Corps to call off the rescue operations until the next day.

"It's got too dark," said Diaz. "And the damned winds are worse than ever. So we'd better pitch our tent right away."

"You can sleep inside with us," said Zervino. "There's plenty of room."

"We'd better not," said Lucero, almost too quickly, as if he'd anticipated the not-too-enticing invitation. "We're supposed to stay on guard outside."

"How about you, Corporal?"

"I've got the same orders," said Bravo. "But I certainly appreciate the offer."

Nevertheless, when the four rescuers had finished arranging their tent and sleeping bags, they joined the eight survivors inside the fuselage shortly after sundown, inhaling huge gulps of fresh air before entering.

"The putrid stench seemed worse at night," Bravo later recalled. "Or maybe it was because we stayed longer. The first time, we went in and out. But this second time we stayed four or five hours, and I could almost feel that odor seeping into my pores—like someone who works in a pigpen."

Yet Bravo and the three alpinists somehow managed to adapt themselves to the penetrating smells. Sitting side by side with the young Uruguayans, ignoring the strips of flesh overhead, they heard the whole story, from the crash to the rescue. The survivors would occasionally lapse into awkward silences that made the darkness oppressive.

"What will they think of us?" asked Delgado, during one of the more prolonged pauses. "Will they really understand? Or will they call us cannibals and savages?"

"I think they'll understand," said Diaz, leaning forward to get a better view of Delgado's silhouetted face. "You did what was necessary, Alfredo. I would do the same thing. *But perhaps it would be better not to talk about it. Why should anyone know?*"

"They're bound to know, Sergio. Any doctor would guess how we survived."

"But I don't think they'll talk about it. And none of us will say anything. Lucero, Villegas, Bravo, and I will promise never to say a word about what we've seen up here."

"You've got to make some kind of report, Sergio. The authorities will ask for it."

"But such reports are always confidential. They're not supposed to be publicized."

As a law student who was also an avid reader of newspapers and magazines, Delgado had little reason to

believe that any government officials could keep a
secret, so he merely shrugged his shoulders when Diaz
repeated his assurance that their report would be strictly confidential.

"We shall see," he said with a knowing smile.

VII

". . . But Don't Talk About It"

While the second group of survivors spent their last
night on the mountaintop, chatting until dawn with
members of the rescue team, Fernando Parrado and
seven others were spending a sleepless night at an ancient hospital in San Fernando, a picturesque provincial
capital 120 miles south of Santiago. At midafternoon,
the helicopter had taken them to a local military base,
from which they had been transferred to the hospital in
two ambulances. Thousands of well-wishers, many of
them from surrounding villages and farms, had jammed
both sides of the tree-lined thoroughfares to greet them,
waving hats and handkerchiefs and shouting *"Viva!"*
and *"Bravo!"* and *"Macanudo che!"*

Glancing through the windshield of the slow-moving
ambulance, Parrado could see hundreds of grinning
faces and tear-filled eyes—old men shaking their heads
in disbelief, grandmotherly women daubing their eyes,
younger people yelling till their faces reddened and
their temples throbbed, and wildly excited children running alongside the ambulances with fresh peaches and
pears in their outstretched hands, shouting, "For you!
For you!"

"It's like a carnival," said one of the survivors to the
driver. "Like an instant holiday—and it's all for us.
What beautiful people!"

They were given a different kind of reception when they arrived at the wall-enclosed patio of the century-old hospital, where more than a hundred reporters and photographers were waiting to question them about every aspect of their miraculous survival. They, too, were friendly and effusive, but their admiration was inevitably mixed with a journalistic hunger for the facts behind the facts. Swarming around the ambulances even before they came to a full stop near the rear door of the emergency clinic, the more aggressive reporters began shouting their congratulations in one breath and asking questions in the next:

"How did you survive?"

"How did the others die?"

"What did you eat?"

"Who was the leader?"

"What did you find to eat up there?"

"How did the women die?"

"Where did you sleep?"

"How did you avoid starving to death?"

"How much weight did you lose?"

Mercifully, for the rather baffled and weary Uruguayans, none of the questions had to be answered at the moment. The doctors and soldiers who had accompanied them quickly formed a wedge-shaped phalanx around the eight arrivals and escorted them through the crowd, politely pushing aside the newsmen and promising them a formal press conference later on—"this evening or tomorrow morning."

Inside the emergency room they were given a warm welcome by the director, Dr. Fernando Baquedano, a scholarly, heavyset man whose delicately molded facial features were almost submerged in puffy clean-shaven cheeks. With fatherly concern, he carefully explained the procedure he had planned since early morning.

"First of all, you'll be given a complete physical examination—head to toe—by my staff of doctors, nurses, and medical technicians. Then, unless you have skin infections, you may take a shower or bath, or simply take a rest if you're not up to it. Then, after

we've taken you to your assigned rooms, you may visit
with your parents and relatives in the visiting salon."

Working with clockwork efficiency while still maintaining an amiable attitude, Dr. Baquedano and his colleagues (Doctors Sergio Valenzuela, Jose Ansin and
Jose Melej) performed various neurological and ortho-
pedic tests, then directed the eight men through a series
of laboratory tests administered by nurses and technicians.

"And it was during those preliminary examinations
that my colleagues and I quickly realized that something
unusual had happened," Dr. Baquedano said later.
"Knowing, as most Chileans do, that there is no source
of food in the high Andes, we had expected to find
these young men in much worse condition. We had
thought they would be in a state of advanced deteriora-
tion—emaciated, dehydrated, mentally deranged, perhaps. But here they were, alert and physically able, with
little or no signs of the acute malnutrition one would
anticipate."

"But quite thin?"

"Oh, yes, they were awfully skinny, some of them
having lost almost half their normal weight. You would
expect that. But they were not malnourished to any
significant degree. They had somehow managed to procure the necessary organic compounds, the crucial
nutrients that the body must have to keep on living.
And protein is the most important of these. Consequently, since there were no animals, plants, birds, or fish at
that high altitude, we had to conclude that they had
eaten human flesh—their only possible source of proteins."

But neither Baquedano nor any of his colleagues
gave any indication at the time of what they knew.
Avoiding any questions about food, they finished their
examinations and sent the eight young patients to their
rooms in the geriatric wing of the hospital, the regular
elderly patients having been temporarily relocated in
other wards. Showering as quickly as possible, Parrado
put on a white cotton smock and cardboard slippers,

hastily combed his hair and beard, and rushed out to the visitors' salon to see his father, older sister, and brother-in-law.

"Papa! Papa!" he yelled as he spotted his father talking with three other parents. *"Aqui estoy, Papa!"*

"Nando, hijo mio!"

With heartrending sobs tearing from his throat, Fernando grabbed his father in a bear hug and scooped him off the floor. "I'm okay, Dad! I'm okay," he kept saying. "I can still pick you up."

Then he hugged his sister and brother-in-law, tears clouding his eyes as he repeated their names over and over again. But suddenly all four of them fell into an awkward silence, aware of a painful reality none of them could bring himself to mention—the tragic deaths of Eugenia and Susana Parrado.

"I tried to save them, Papa," said Fernando in a choked whisper. "I tried with all my heart and all my strength—and I pleaded with God to let them live, to take me instead. . . ."

"I know, Fernando—I know you tried," said his father, tears streaming down his cheeks. "But there was nothing you could do, son. I guess it was God's will that—"

His voice broke off in a sob as Fernando once again embraced him, both of them overwhelmed by a grief no words could express. "My son, my son, my son," was all his father could say; and Fernando's only response was, "Papa, Papa, Papa."

It was later reported that Seler Parrado had flown to Chile on the first available plane, knowing that his son had survived and still hoping that his wife and teen-age daughter had also been found alive. Like most of the parents, he had read the list of survivors in a Montevideo newspaper but nevertheless clung to the prayer that it was erroneous or incomplete. Apparently, not until he saw the expression on his son's face when they first met in San Fernando was he finally convinced they had died.

Several other parents whose sons were not on the

list of survivors had also flown to Santiago and then taken taxis to San Fernando, praying all the way that there had been a mistake in the published reports. They simply refused to believe their sons had died until they heard it directly from one of the eight men who came on the first helicopter.

"I'm terribly sorry, *senora*—but I must tell you that Daniel did not survive. He died in the crash." Or, "I'm sorry, *senor,* but Diego died in the avalanche."

Stunned by the final confirmation of what they had actually known to be true but had stubbornly refused to believe, the mothers would stare blankly around the reception salon, mumbling the son's name and then bursting into sobs as their husbands tried desperately to comfort them, momentarily containing their own grief with lips clamped tight as a trap.

But when the reunited parents and sons had finally vented their pent-up feelings, they started joking with each other and mingling with other family groups, as if the older and younger alumni of the Colegio Stella Maris had suddenly decided to hold a reunion. "They had an *esprit de corps* one seldom sees," Dr. Baquedano later observed. "They had obviously known each other a long time, and their ordeal had cemented that relationship forever."

Their spirits were still high (almost giddy in one nurse's opinion) when they sat down for their first regular meal in seventy-two days. Having expected to find the survivors in a state of severe malnutrition, the hospital dietician had planned an extremely bland diet for the first twenty-four hours—tea, consomme, and Jell-O—and the Uruguayans doubled over with laughter when they saw the food trays on their bedside tables.

"You must be kidding," yelled Daniel Fernandez with a boyish giggle. "This is baby food! We're grown men!"

"And we're starving," said Carlos Paez. "Haven't you got some real food?"

"Doctor's orders," said the young nurse who had

brought the trays. "You have to take it easy these first few days."

"But we're okay, *senorita*. We're not really sick. We can eat anything—even a horse."

Remembering that one of them had eaten a flower with a joyous comic gusto, chewing each petal with the dramatic delicacy of a skilled pantomimist, the nurse smiled sweetly and said, "Of course you can—but not today."

"I'll give you my autograph—two autographs—for a ham sandwich," one of them said teasingly. "We're going to be famous, *senorita,* and someday those autographs will be worth a dollar apiece. Maybe a dollar and a half!"

"Probably a hundred dollars," she said. "But you can't bribe me."

But an hour later, after the chief dietician had talked with the medical director, the men were served green beans and noodles with a light egg batter, a favorite local dish.

Meanwhile, two or three informal but serious discussions had taken place among Roberto Canessa, Fernando Parrado, and two other survivors who were medical students. "These doctors obviously know that we've eaten meat," Canessa told each one in a soft confidential voice. "They'd have to be incompetent fools not to realize it, especially now that they've examined us."

"Okay, Roberto, we'll grant you that—but what should we do about it?"

"I think we should tell them everything—just as I told Dr. Arriagada on the helicopter—and ask their advice on how to handle the matter."

"I think you're right, Roberto. We haven't done anything wrong, so there's no sense trying to conceal it."

Having established a consensus among the eight survivors at the hospital, Canessa soon thereafter talked at great length with Dr. Baquedano. They sat in the director's large but sparsely furnished office, facing each

other across a modest utilitarian desk of the variety
that one might expect to see in a secretary's cubicle.

"I've something to tell you that you probably know
already," said Canessa after the customary pleasantries.
"But I guess you ought to hear all the details."

Feeling somewhat like a priest about to hear a confession, the doctor simply nodded and leaned back in
his swivel chair as Canessa bent forward, speaking in a
quiet, methodical voice which after a while seemed
rather hypnotic to Baquedano. Step by step, going back
to the first few days after the accident, he talked about
their futile search for food in the frozen wastes of the
cordillera; their growing hunger as their supply of
cheese and chocolate dwindled despite tight rationing
by Roy Harley; how they had decided not to brush their
teeth so they could eat the toothpaste for dessert; the
headaches and dizziness that became especially acute
after the avalanche and the subsequent fights they'd had
when tempers grew short; their fateful conversation with
Dr. Nicola as he was dying; the decision to follow his
advice, and the resistance expressed by some of their
companions.

Even though he had guessed the basic facts, the doctor was nevertheless slightly shaken at first and then
professionally impressed as he listened to the specific
details.

"One has to admire their intelligence, their amazing
resourcefulness," he later commented to several colleagues. "Once they had decided to break that ancient
taboo, they did it with great maturity and wisdom."

Yet there was an edge of anxiety in Canessa's voice,
an unspoken need to be reassured, and Baquedano responded with gentle concern. "You did what you had
to do, Roberto, and you acted with great intelligence.
No one could possibly blame you." Then, as he glanced
through a side window and spotted a photographer on
the roof of an adjacent building, he added the same
warning Canessa had received from Dr. Arriagada:
"But I don't think you should talk about this to any-

one—certainly not to the press. Just keep it to your-
selves, Roberto."

"But how can we keep it a secret? Someone is bound
to find out, Doctor. Just by the simple process of reasoning."

"Not necessarily, Roberto. You'd have to be a doctor
or an expert in nutrition."

"But the reporters keep asking us how we managed
to survive—what we ate and drank—that sort of question. So they must suspect something."

"Let me try to handle that problem. Meanwhile, I'd
suggest that you and your friends avoid any public
discussion about what you ate."

Though apparently reassured by Baquedano's blanket
approval of what they had done, the Uruguayans were
nonetheless puzzled by his advice that they avoid any
mention of their consumption of human flesh. Understandably confused by that obvious contradiction and
perhaps needing further assurance, most of the eight
survivors talked quite freely about their "strange diet"
with the nurses who later attended them. They particularly confided in Ana Astete Percira, the motherly
nurse in charge of their ward.

She was a handsome, rather buxom woman with well-
molded features, moist brown eyes, smooth olive com-
plexion, and wavy black hair tightly pulled back into
a neat bun. About forty-five years old and the mother
of two teen-agers, she had no difficulty communicating
with the young Uruguayans.

"They made no attempt to hide the truth," she later
revealed. "Those youngsters wanted everyone to know.
It was as if they felt compelled to purge themselves—
to confess everything. And we kept assuring them that
they had done no wrong, had committed no sin. I told
them that I would have been happy to sacrifice my own
body if I had been one of the deceased. Some of them
cried when I said that. They hugged me as if I were
their own mother, and I was terribly moved by their
reaction. They were like little boys wanting to be told
that everything was all right now, that they were really

loved and forgiven. It almost tore me apart inside because I knew how desperately they needed understanding and genuine forgiveness."

But she also felt it necessary to caution them not to talk about what they had done, not to mention it to anyone else. Judging from their subsequent behavior, the young Uruguayans must have got the same advice from the priest who heard their confessions and gave them holy communion at a special mass that same evening. Although no one knows what is actually said in the privacy of the confessional, one can easily surmise that the priest also guaranteed them they had committed no sin, that they indeed had a moral obligation not to let themselves starve to death—but nevertheless advised them not to talk about it to anyone else. Whether it was an immediate reaction to his priestly advice or the euphoric ambience of the mass itself, Parrado and his seven companions seemed calmer when they returned to their rooms.

"They were not subdued, mind you—just more relaxed," Senora Astete later remembered. "But, of course, some of them were still in a prankish mood, especially Carlitos Pacz. We caught him sneaking out of the kitchen with a loaf of bread and a big sausage; but he merely laughed when my assistant blocked his way. I'm sure he expected to be caught."

According to most of the nurses, Carlitos was the most amiable of the group—easygoing, charming, irrepressibly friendly. Canessa was the most aloof and "sort of watchful, like a sleek panther guarding all approaches." But Fernando Parrado was the most puzzling—friendly one moment and then suddenly remote. "He would be telling us about something that happened on the cordillera, smiling like a happy young boy and gesturing with his hands—then, suddenly, he would break away in the middle of a sentence, his eyes staring through or beyond us, his hands slumping to his lap."

"Excuse me," he would say. "I have to go now." Then he would walk away from the inside patio to the deserted back terrace, his eyes still distant, his chapped

lips slightly parted as if he were about to answer a
question that only he had heard. "He was," Dr. Baquedano later concluded, "an instinctive loner, a man who
can be gracious when it's necessary, but who requires
a great deal of solitude. And strangely enough, this apparent aloofness is a crucial factor in his becoming a
natural leader, because this need to be alone makes
him seem remote and somehow mysterious, as if he
knows something no one else knows. And that's why
people are willing to follow Parrado. By doing so, they
think they'll get to know what he knows; and of course,
they never will."

"But there's one more factor to consider," said the
chief nurse. "They also knew that Fernando has an
incredible will to survive. Who else could have lived
through a three-day coma in freezing weather at that
altitude? Surely, his friends must have thought he was
some kind of miracle man, someone especially en-
dowed by the gods themselves. Then, having survived
that ordeal and the deaths of his mother and sister, he
was still the strongest among them—physically and
psychologically—so it was almost inevitable that he
would be the one to make that final ten-day journey
that would have been impossible for anyone else."

Yet, in spite of their great admiration, Baquedano
and Astete wondered if Parrado would be able to withstand the incessant needling pressures against him and
his companions during the next few days by the hundred or more reporters and photographers who were
waiting outside the hospital like hungry jackals. The
director had managed to appease them, at least temporarily, by promising a formal press conference on the
following morning, but he had been unable to ward off
the hundreds of phone calls from parents, relatives,
government officials, and journalists pleading for information from editorial offices in Santiago, Montevideo,
Buenos Aires, Paris, New York, Lima, Rome, Tokyo,
Berlin, Mexico City, and several other capitals. "Suddenly our peaceful little town had become world-
famous. But most of those long-distance calls gave me

a sense of foreboding, an awful queasiness in the pit of my stomach, because they kept asking me the same damned question: 'What did they eat to stay alive, Doctor?' So I'd pretend that I couldn't hear them because of a faulty connection, or I'd simply tell them there would be a press conference tomorrow morning."

Concealing his anxiety, Dr. Baquedano spent two or three hours chatting with the survivors in their rooms or in the visitors' lounge, where most of them assembled after taking hour-long baths.

"What shall we do with their clothes?" asked one of the younger nurses. "They smell awful. I don't think anyone can ever get them clean again."

"I guess you'll have to burn them," said the director. "One of our local merchants has already offered to bring them new clothes tomorrow morning."

Wearing new trousers, shirts, and shoes—some of them clean-shaven for the first time in two months— six of the survivors appeared for the press conference shortly before noon of the following day. The meeting was held in a side patio outside the recreation lounge, a soft summer breeze rustling the thick leaves of a fan-shaped palmetto and the slender eucalyptus on the far side of the adjacent garden. Standing on either side of Dr. Baquedano were Fernando Parrado, Roberto Canessa, Carlos Paez, Daniel Fernandez, Eduardo Strauch, and Pedro Algorta, their gaunt faces and emaciated, but proudly erect, figures framed by the gray weatherworn adobe wall behind them. Several nurses and male ward attendants, all dressed in white, leaned through half-open windows or stood near the glass doors, their eyes shifting from the young men they'd learned to love to the restless crowding-in reporters who might expose them to pain and anguish.

Probably more attuned to that possible trauma than most of his staff, Dr. Baquedano opened the conference with a few preliminary remarks that he hoped would discourage the questions he wanted to evade. "As you probably realize, these youngsters have been through a terrible ordeal from which they have not entirely recovered, either physically or psychologically. Consequently, although I appreciate your need to find out as much as you can, I hope you'll understand that they're not quite ready to discuss all aspects of this truly horrifying experience—the painful suffering and eventual deaths of relatives and dear friends and their own suffering as well. So I'd like to ask them to tell you what they are able to tell you at this particular time, and that you refrain from asking questions that may evoke too much anxiety."

Then, after having explained that Jose Inciarte and Alvaro Mangino would be unable to participate in the conference on account of medical reasons, he introduced Fernando Parrado.

"I haven't much to say," he began in a soft but firm voice. "Nothing much to add to what Roberto and I have already said to some of you. But I guess the most difficult part of this adventure was our final ten-day trip through all that snow and ice. As Roberto will tell you, it wasn't very easy. But, of course, we couldn't have succeeded without the help of all the others. They were the ones—Carlos, Eduardo, Alfredo, Alvaro, and all the rest—they were the ones who made our sleeping bags and climbing equipment and also gave us their rations. It was all a team effort, and I shall always be proud to have been with them. Because they have all been terribly brave and also very ingenious, incredibly inventive in finding ways to stay alive under the worst circumstances. And, of course, I want to thank Sergio Catalan and all the fine Chilean people who came to rescue us and risked their lives doing so. Last of all, we want to thank Dr. Baquedano and his wonderful staff for their great kindness and understanding."

After a brief round of applause (and before anyone could ask any questions), Baquedano introduced Carlos Paez, who talked about the "very strict rationing of an estimated ninety pounds of chocolate and four hundred pounds of cheese which we'd got during our stopover in Mendoza."

"That's an awful lot of chocolate and cheese to pick up on a mere stopover," someone remarked.

"Well, I guess it was, but we'd heard such items were in short supply here in Chile, so we brought our own."

"And what did you eat after you'd exhausted your chocolate and cheese?"

"We managed to find certain roots and fungus plants —lichen and mushrooms—under and between the rocks. They tasted awful at first, but after a while they seemed delicious. We made soup from them, using anything we could find for fuel. I even burned some postcards that I'd bought for some of my Chilean friends."

There were no other questions about food, and the rest of the press conference was devoted to brief statements about various other activities, with Strauch and Fernandez answering most of the questions. Then Canessa made a brief statement about his duties as "medical director" and answered several queries about the emergency surgery he had performed, but carefully avoided any reference to problems of nutrition.

When the conference was over and the reporters safely out of sight, Dr. Baquedano turned toward his head nurse and drew a deep sigh of relief. "It got kind of rough for a moment, Ana, but I guess they did all right."

"Those reporters were feeling very kind and sort of sentimental today," she said with a weary smile. "But I'm wondering how long they will stay that way. After all, Doctor, cannibalism can be quite a sensational story, and sensationalism is what most journalists live on."

"I guess you're right, Ana, but maybe they'll be a little more gentle in this particular case. These boys already face a terrible psychological problem—even if it's never publicized. I sure hope these journalists realize how much harm they can cause—and that they'll finally decide to leave the boys alone."

Unfortunately, certain reporters felt a contrary obligation. About an hour after the press conference, one of them cornered Alvaro Mangino in a hospital corridor and pointedly asked him about the "lichen soup" Paez had mentioned.

"Well, the lichen wasn't anything special," he answered, unaware of what Paez had said since he himself had not participated in the conference. "We ate lichen only one time, just one single day that I can remember. We dug the lichen out of some moss under a rock, but it was so darned far away—the place where we found it—that it wasn't worth the trouble hiking all that distance for something that had very little food value. So we gave up on the lichen."

Meanwhile, in a different section of the hospital, another eager reporter was interviewing Jose Inciarte, who had also missed the press conference. Confined to a wheelchair and feeling slightly nauseous, he answered only a few questions, one of which related to his special duties as "chief investigator of botanical food sources." Fully supporting Paez' statement, he also declared that "lichen and other roots" had been an important part of their regular food supply.

Apparently assuming that Paez' "lichen soup" had seemed rather unsubstantial to the skeptical reporters, Parrado later told another reporter that they had also eaten birds and fish, which they'd got from the lake at the base of the volcano. "We killed the birds with slingshots, which we made from the elastic bands on our ski pants," he explained.

Either out of ignorance or kindness, the correspondent never pressed him for details; nor did he mention in his subsequent article that no one had ever seen any kind of bird or fish at that altitude.

Consequently, although most reporters jealously guard whatever tidbits they manage to gather through their individual efforts, several of the newsmen at San Fernando began to compare notes and to wonder aloud about what the survivors had really eaten to stay alive for seventy-two days in a region that had no source of food. But when they sought answers to that question from the doctors who had talked with the survivors, they got little or no satisfaction.

Dr. Eduardo Arriagada, the army surgeon who made the preliminary examination of the first group of survivors (those who were taken to the San Fernando hospital), merely deepened the mystery when he was interviewed by Jorge Argomedo for *La Prensa*. "When I first talked to them," he said, "the thing that impressed me most was their fine spirit, and the fact that they'd managed to survive at all under such adverse conditions. They were all in good physical shape, but their mental alertness was even more remarkable—truly admirable. When our helicopter came into view, they were absolutely euphoric, jumping up and down and shouting, laughing and hugging each other—incredibly animated.

"My first physical examination clearly showed that they were all in an advanced stage of malnutrition, most of them having lost forty or fifty pounds, but the nourishment they'd got during those seventy-two days in the mountains had given them extraordinary strength.

"As for the nutriments ingested during that period, there is little that I can say—because all that pertains to a secret official report. But the explanation of how they managed to survive until now, against such adversity—well, that you will have to find in some realm outside the scope of medicine or any other science. Until now we have no logical explanation. The answer escapes any known scientific criteria. And if I were not a doctor I would have to believe it was a miracle."

Pressed for a more exact statement, the doctor simply shrugged and repeated himself. "I can't tell you any more about what they ate. That's part of a confidential report. The important thing to remember is that they *did* survive—that they've been reunited with their loved ones."

Needless to say, such statements were bound to arouse further suspicions. Who had written the "confidential official report" that Dr. Arriagado had so mysteriously mentioned? To whom was it directed—the Air Force, the Police, the Minister of Foreign Affairs, the Attorney General? Would the report be released

later on? And if not, who could be bribed to provide a
Xerox copy of it? But, most important of all—what did
the report contain that caused it to be classified as "confidential"?

With these and many other unanswered questions
churning inside them, the army of journalists hopped
into their cars and taxicabs to follow the survivors and
their families on an impromptu motorcade to Santiago
at midafternoon, some of the photographers shuttling
back and forth to snap pictures through car windows,
brashly ignoring any pleas for privacy. The farewell at
the hospital was typically Latin—warm embraces from
doctors, nurses, and ward attendants, solemnly repeated
promises to come back soon, and heartfelt wishes for
good luck.

In a burst of euphoric gratitude, Carlos Paez' artist
father promised to paint a huge mural on the walls of
the visitors' lounge. There were further displays of af-
fection and admiration from the local townspeople as
they drove through the tree-shaded main thoroughfare,
several children tagging along and reaching for a farewell handshake from the heroes of the Andes. And
when Inciarte and Mangino came by in an army ambulance, still under medical supervision, there was an
instant chorus of *bravos* and *oles,* accompanied by
quickly gathered bouquets of roses, azaleas, and mari-
golds tossed from all angles. Parrado, Canessa, Strauch,
Algorta, Paez, and Fernandez, riding with their parents
in several different cars, were also cheered and show-
ered with flowers as they came to a crowded intersection
and turned north onto the highway leading to the
Chilean capital.

The eight remaining survivors, having just been rescued by helicopter and transported to the military base
for a brief stopover, were also on their way to Santiago.
They were accompanied by an Air Force doctor named
Eduardo Sanchez, with whom they spoke at great length
about every aspect of their prolonged ordeal in what
one of them described as "an ice-covered hell." He was
particularly impressed by their eagerness, their compel-

ling need, to explain their decision to eat the flesh of their dead companions. "There was no attempt to conceal anything," he later told his colleagues. "So I assured them they had done no wrong, that they had no other choice." But he, too, urged them not to talk about it, not to mention anything to the press or even their friends.

And when they finally arrived at the government hospital in Santiago, they got the same advice from the scholarly, white-haired director, Dr. Raul Zapata. Among the most brilliant doctors in Chile, the sixty-year-old surgeon has a gentle father-confessor demeanor that invites confidence. Calling upon his staff of specialists, he immediately ordered complete "head-to-toe and inside-out" examinations, with laboratory tests of blood, urine, and saliva, meanwhile chatting with each of the men and personally observing that they were in "remarkably good shape" considering what they had been through.

Just as Dr. Baquedano had surmised the truth about his eight patients at San Fernando, Dr. Zapata instantly realized that the survivors who had come to his hospital had consumed enough proteins to avoid the ravages of extreme malnutrition. Thus, when they freely admitted what they had already told Cpl. Bravo, the three alpinists, and Dr. Sanchez, the director merely nodded like a wise old grandfather listening to a favorite grandchild explaining why he'd dropped out of college in his sophomore year. Their anxious eyes were begging for assurance, for confirmation that they had committed no evil, that their parents and friends (and fiancees) would understand.

"Do you think they'll *really* understand, Doctor?"

"Of course they will. After all, you've done nothing to be ashamed of, nothing to feel guilty about."

Nevertheless, he felt the need to add the seemingly-inevitable caveat: "But I don't think you should mention this to anyone else."

Then, in a gallant effort to foreclose any further discussion of what had become a tantalizing mystery,

Dr. Zapata tried to enlist the cooperation of the press itself at a subsequent news conference attended by seven of the Uruguayans in starchy white hospital smocks, their putrid, sweaty clothes and shoes having been tossed into the hospital incinerator while they bathed. First introducing himself and the young men, he asked the reporters to refrain from asking any questions relating to what kind of food the survivors had eaten.

"I know how curious you are about every facet of this struggle for survival, but I hope you'll understand that certain things happened that are too painful to remember or to talk about. These boys have been through agonies most of us will never know; and therefore—as their medical supervisor and, more importantly, as their friend—I must ask you not to delve into the question of nutrition. And I hope we can have a gentleman's agreement to spare them any further anguish in this regard."

Glancing at each other and then at the expectant expressions on the gaunt faces of the seven undernourished and skeleton-thin survivors, the usually blase reporters seemingly accepted Zapata's injunction, most of them nodding affirmatively. "I felt like a softhearted boob," one of them later remarked in the bar of the Sheraton Hotel, "and I was glad to feel that way."

There were, however, three or four reporters whose emotions were less binding than their journalistic curiosity.

VIII

The Second Avalanche

Having now confided in six doctors and two priests—all of them certifiable "father figures" in the most classical sense—the sixteen survivors found themselves in a state of torturous confusion caused by their mentors' uniformly contrary advice: *"You've done no wrong—but don't admit it."*

"If we've done nothing to feel guilty about, why should we keep it a dark secret?"

"Is it possible to keep it a secret now that we've told so many people?"

"And what will happen if and when the truth comes out? How shall we explain our attempts to conceal it?"

Such were the dilemmas that hounded fourteen of the Uruguayans when they checked into the suburban Hotel Sheraton San Cristobal immediately after they had been released from the hospital.

Lounging around the beautiful outdoor swimming pool in bathing trunks that hung loosely on their bony hips, the much publicized and constantly photographed group were the objects of the curiosity and effusive admiration of hundreds of hotel guests and local visitors who swarmed through the huge lobby and the outside patios from early morning till after midnight. Among them were scores of beautiful mini-skirted and flirtatious *senoritas* from nearby upper-class residential areas, providing ample evidence that Chilean women are the most liberated and least inhibited females in Latin America.

Undoubtedly reflecting the more traditional conservatism of her native Uruguay, Roberto Canessa's lovely young fiancee, Laura Sacurra, audibly wondered what would have happened if she had not been with Roberto to help him resist their "outrageous advances." But those who lacked such devoted protection were pleased to accept the affectionate attention of the sophisticated *senoritas*.

But not everyone was in a carefree holiday mood. On the far side of the pool, sitting on the edge with his thin, pale legs dangling in the cool water, one of the younger survivors was immersed in a soul-searching conversation with his twenty-year-old fiancee. He had told her about their "difficult decision" and the subsequent anguish they'd suffered, how Numa Turcatti had preferred to die rather than eat the meat pellets, and how everyone kept saying they'd done no wrong but still cautioned them to keep quiet about it, and did she really understand—"or are you just saying that to be kind?" And she chokingly, tearfully telling him, "Of course I understand! And I'll still love you no matter what anybody says."

Meanwhile, Fernando Parrado was being interviewed by an Argentine television correspondent on the dining terrace nearby, both slouched on the soft plastic cushions of white wrought-iron chairs, elbows casually resting on the glass-topped table. Apparently heedful of Dr. Zapata's injunction, the Argentinian talked around the question of food, Parrado warily and wearily repeating much of what he had already said in prior interviews, his eyes occasionally fixed on the snow-capped peaks of the dazzling cordillera that loomed over the city. "They're awfully big," he said, momentarily straying from the question he'd just been asked. "It hardly seems possible that we hiked and climbed through all those mountains."

"Well, now that you've mentioned that final ten-day hike, Fernando—why did Antonio Vicintin quit and go back after you'd got to the top of the volcano?"

"He didn't quit. That was *my* suggestion. Antonio wanted to stay with us—all the way. But when we got

to the top of El Tinguiririca and realized we had under-
estimated how long we had to travel and that we would
probably run out of food, I asked Antonio to go back
so that Roberto and I could use his rations."

An awkward silence then, the Argentinian logically
wanting to ask what kind of rations they had taken
along, but deliberately avoiding that line of inquiry, and
Parrado no doubt wondering if one could ever evade
the tantalizing question that seemed to hover over every
interview.

Several miles away, at the studios of the EMELCO
television film company, Antonio Vicintin was also
being interviewed, for a soon-to-be-released documen-
tary. But his interlocutor, Alvaro Covacevich, probably
knew more about the facts behind the news than most
reporters or commentators. As producer-narrator of
several documentaries for President Salvador Allende's
administration, Covacevich had got permission to send
his chief cameraman as the only film photographer or
reporter on either of the two Air Force helicopters that
participated in the first rescue mission. Consequently,
his company had about three minutes of motion picture
footage of the dismembered limbs scattered near the
fuselage of the wrecked plane. But he, too, refrained
from asking Vicintin the forbidden question. "I felt we
all had a moral duty to follow Dr. Zapata's suggestion,"
he later told an associate. "But I was also convinced
that it was a secret which couldn't be kept. Too many
people knew already, and there seemed to be an awful
lot of bribe money floating around."

It was rumored, for example, that *Paris Match* magazine had paid $50,000 for a couple of rolls of color
photographs taken by one of the survivors during the
long sojourn in the cordillera. Instantly calculating in
terms of black-market *escudos,* Chilean reporters
started talking about 21,000,000 *escudos,* then further
breaking it down to 21 billion *pesos.* Latin-American
headline writers frequently resort to this numerical
folderol to jazz up otherwise pedestrian news; but, even
when left unconverted into funny money, fifty thousand

dollars was a considerable sum to invest in just ordinary pictures, so it was logically assumed that the photographs were full of sensational revelations.

With that rumor as an appetizer, the hundred or more reporters had something to chew on as they milled around the Sheraton, hoping to catch an impromptu remark from one of the survivors or from a close friend or relative. "This hotel has a million ears," remarked a red-jacketed waiter to a pretty cashier. "Everyone seems to be eavesdropping on everyone else's conversation." But there were also less covert exchanges of rumors and speculations among the more pensive members of the foreign press. Huddled together in the dark recesses of the indoor cocktail lounge, meditatively sipping their frothy Pisco Sours or the far more expensive bourbon-on-the-rocks, they spent hours trying to make head or tail of the "official confidential report" which Dr. Arriagada had so elusively mentioned. One of them hinted that a fellow correspondent had got a Xerox copy of the disputed report and that a "pretty sensational story" would be breaking into print within a couple of days in one of the principal newspapers outside Chile or Uruguay. Another mentioned an interview with Dr. Eduardo Sanchez, in which he kept insisting that the Uruguayans' principal problem would be of a psychiatric nature, once again raising the supicion that a great deal had been left unsaid.

Perhaps unaware of the controversy swirling around them, most of the fourteen survivors left the hotel at midafternoon to shop for new clothes and Christmas presents. As they went from one store to another, they were besieged by small and then larger groups of well-wishers and autograph-seekers who quickly recognized them, their pictures having been spread across front pages throughout Chile. "It's another instant carnival," remarked a female reporter who had accompanied them. "The whole world loves them. They're heroes." Some of the storekeepers who served them were suddenly smitten by the contagious Christmas Eve euphoria and reduced their prices to wholesale levels or simply refused to accept any money from the survivors. But they readily accepted autographs, and some of them photographed the Uruguayans standing in front of their stores with their tired arms raised in the universal V-for-victory salute. Thus acquiring armloads of bargains and gifts, they returned to the hotel in the gayest of moods, some of them singing and laughing like young schoolboys as they rode the crowded elevators up to their rooms.

A few hours later, as thousands of Chilean families gathered around brightly decorated trees and fireplaces to celebrate Christmas Eve, ten of the survivors, their families, close friends, and a few journalists attended a dinner in the elegant Salon Cochrane on the hotel mezzanine. Those present were Parrado, Inciarte, Vicintin, Paez, Algorta, Zervino, Delgado, Sabella, and the two Strauch brothers. Roy Harley and Javier Methol, both suffering from persistent illness, were confined in their rooms. Francois, Mangino, and Fernandez had returned to Montevideo, and Canessa was visiting old friends in Santiago.

For those at the banquet there were hot hors d'oeuvres, champagne and sparkling burgundy, and a sumptuous spread of turkey, ham, roast beef, several kinds of cheese, deviled eggs, olives, sweet pickles, potato salad, hot rolls, chilled vegetables, French pastries, and fresh berries, all appetizingly displayed in the flickering light of tall red candles in gleaming silver candelabra. It should have been a joyous occasion, yet an aura of sadness permeated the brightly decorated room. Christmas being a time for fond remembrance, the young Uruguayans were no doubt thinking of old friends who had not survived the terrifying accident and prolonged misery that followed it. So there were numerous sudden and profound silences, abrupt pauses in mid-conversation, eyes fading out of focus, and anxious, overattentive mothers jabbering to fill an awkward void, tentatively (almost shyly) reaching out to touch their sons' hair as if to smooth down a vagrant cowlick, asking again and again, "Are you all right?

Are you all right? Are you all right?" Not daring to touch nor to ask the small questions women use as caresses rather than questions, their more taciturn husbands merely stood to one side (mostly for fear of being rebuffed), clearing their throats and anxious to drink more than seemed approriate.

Unfettered by such parental fears of rejection and having no generation gap to bridge, the survivors' young Chilean friends thought nothing of breaking into awkward silences with forced jokes and teasing camaraderie. Alfredo Delgado, with a painful limp resulting from an imperfectly healed fracture, was a natural butt for locker-room humor; and so was Jose Inciarte, who had just abandoned his wheelchair. Respecting, perhaps envying that youthful rapport, the few journalists present patiently nursed their drinks, nibbled their canapes, chain-smoked expensive American cigarettes obtained from friendly diplomats, and watchfully recorded the drama, like silent cameras.

One of those human cameras had already recorded a father-son episode that clearly reflected the nervous tension which seemed to be on the increase among the Uruguayans. Carlos Paez, Jr., apparently feeling that the reporters were being neglected, had got involved in a friendly chat with one of them. But his usually garrulous father, who had been assiduously courting the press and garnering considerable publicity for himself, suddenly broke in on his son's conversation and warned him not to talk about his experiences, not "to rake over old coals." Annoyed by the interruption and perhaps feeling that Papa was once again pushing into stage center, young Paez whisked around and angrily told him to shut up. And when the older Paez persisted, Carlos threatened to punch him in the nose.

"Try it, if you think you can," said his father, squaring off. "I've waited all this time to see you, and now you want to punch my face."

Fortunately, several friends immediately stepped between them and finally restored a measure of grudging civility between them. Some observers attributed the son's angry threat to the war of nerves that had been developing between the survivors and the press; others surmised that Carlos, Jr., had become increasingly embarrassed and resentful of his father's continual efforts to steal the limelight. He might have been thinking of the incredibly egotistical note which Carlos, Sr., had sent him via the pilot of the rescue helicopter.

Hola, Carlitos Miguel! As you can see, I've never failed you. I'm sending you this helicopter as a Christmas present. Mama arrives today in San Fernando. Hugs and kisses.

The Old Man

Whatever Carlos, Jr., may have felt afterward about his sudden outburst, he never conveyed it to the press. But his father was quick to apologize for his son's behavior and asked reporters to bear in mind "the enormous psychological pressures that all these boys have been undergoing."

Near midnight they heard muted explosions of firecrackers, church bells tolling, and several voices singing Christmas carols on the terrace below the banquet room. Pausing in their conversations to listen to the outside noises, the survivors rushed toward each other and embraced with tears streaming down their cheeks.

They were singing a song when Cesar Charlone Ortego, Charge d'Affaires of the Uruguayan embassy, arrived with an armload of gifts that had been sent to the boys from numerous Chilean admirers. He also gave them a religious plaque for the Colegio Stella Maris. Soon thereafter, clearly exhausted by a night too weighted with mixed emotions, they began straggling out of the salon and back to their rooms.

Just outside the doorway, the Uruguayan reporter momentarily delayed Antonio Vicintin, who was leaving alone. "I forgot to tell you," he said with a friendly smile, "that your brother Alvaro came to my office at *El Dia* with your obituary about two months after the accident. But we didn't publish it because some of us had a hunch that there might be a few survivors."

"You must be kidding," said Vicintin with a slight chuckle. "How I wish Alvarito were here—I really miss him. But it would have been more amusing if you'd gone ahead and published my obituary."

Next day, they attended a special Christmas mass, all of them receiving holy communion from Monsignor Raul Hasbun, who told the congregation that the young Uruguayans' survival had been "a gift from God."

Leaving the chapel, they were surrounded by hundreds of Chileans who had come to pray with and for them, and one of them tearfully remarked that "we are completely at home in Santiago. No one could possibly treat us with more kindness than the wonderful people of Chile."

He might have qualified that remark if he had seen the front page of *El Clarin,* a multicolored tabloid, that appeared on local newsstands as the mass was ending. Under a lurid red headline above a bright yellow square superimposed on black type, the lead article announced that "the international press has broadcast a terrible revelation all over the world. And the hard truth seems to be that cannibalism saved the sixteen survivors who struggled to survive against the fury of nature."

El Clarin was referring to sensational stories published that same day in Buenos Aires, Lima, and Paris. Without further elaboration on what had been said in the foreign press, *El Clarin* explained its own editorial ambivalence as follows:

The Chilean reporters had tried to investigate the details of this incredible occurrence, having been in San Fernando as well as the pre-cordillera, and they had asked the survivors certain specific questions. But their *noblesse oblige,* due to the weakened condition of the young men, restrained them from pressing for more exact details when the Uruguayans kept giving them evasive answers. And why should they pursue the question? In the final analysis, the only thing that really mattered was their being alive. . . .

Apparently, none of the survivors read *El Clarín* that day, or they chose to ignore it. They returned to the hotel for lunch and then scattered about to take in the sights of Santiago or to visit local friends. Meanwhile, the rumors were accumulating into a monstrous avalanche that was rumbling all around them, a journalistic avalanche that could be far more damaging than the one they had survived on the cordillera.

IX

The Journalistic Nightmare

On the day after Christmas, an afternoon newspaper sent more shock waves throughout Santiago with the most sensational news story ever printed in Chile. In banner headlines covering half the front page, *La Segunda* revealed what many reporters had known for several days:

MAY GOD FORGIVE THEM!

CANNIBALISM JUSTIFIED

THE LOGICAL AND HIDDEN TRUTH HAS BEEN REVEALED ABOUT THE SURVIVORS OF THE AIR CRASH: THEY SURVIVED BY EATING THE BODIES OF THEIR DEAD COMPANIONS. QUERY: WHAT WOULD YOU HAVE DONE?

"On the fourth day we started hiking through the mountains to see if we could find something to eat.

We had already consumed all the food we could salvage from the plane. But the only thing we found was a measly weed, which was difficult to reach under all that snow. We came, at that moment, to the terrible realization that the mountains would not provide us with the food necessary for survival. And it was then that we made the dramatic decision: In order to survive, we had to overcome whatever obstacle, whatever religious or biological barrier confronted us. And, thanks to that decision, we're alive."

This statement was made to this newspaper this morning by one of the survivors of the Uruguayan plane that crashed in the cordillera. It confirms a rumor that has been circulating everywhere during the past weekend, and which today became an explosive reality in the Chilean press. Newspapers in Lima and Buenos Aires had already published the report; consequently, we could not—either out of respect or consideration—maintain our silence on this matter.

It is interesting to note that nowhere in the lengthy article did *La Segunda* identify the alleged informant; and the rather stilted language sounds more like an editor pontificating than a young man confessing. But the article itself is here translated in its entirety because it is a typical example of the journalistic nightmare that will haunt the young survivors for—who knows how long?

Our readers will have to reach their own conclusions. Obviously, the revelation of this chilling aspect of the extraordinary feat of the sixteen young rugby stars of the Old Christian Club will shock most people. But although harsh reality is often hard to bear, one must have a cool head to lend a human focus to such events. The circumstances themselves enable us to feel charitable toward these youngsters. Not often does one live

through such an unusual ordeal at two miles above
sea level, surrounded by injured or dead friends,
and facing a miserable loneliness and isolation.
Frustrated in their hopes of being rescued, listening to radio broadcasts announcing that the search
had been abandoned, they were left to the mercy
of Divine Providence and to their own determination to survive.

In such circumstances, what could they do?
Moreover, this isn't the first time this has happened. During the Second World War a squad of
American soldiers found themselves in a similar
situation, completely isolated and abandoned on a
deserted little island in the South Pacific. Without
food and with no hope of being rescued, they did
what they had to do. That's how they managed to
survive until they were finally rescued.

The same thing happened here. Thus, even the
simplest logic dictated a similar solution. But
imagine the psychic trauma they suffered, the terrifying emotional shock that some of them went
through when the majority made that fateful decision. Ignoring the grim details—which may be
worse than anything we can imagine—we seek
only to justify their actions and to hope their
emotional trauma will not be too severe. For beyond any ulterior consideration, it is only fair in
these difficult moments to tell them, "We're happy
that you're alive—and may God forgive you!"

It was later revealed that the Andean Rescue Corps
had made the following report of what it had seen at the
scene of the accident:

"In order to survive for seventy-two days in the
cordillera of the Andes, the survivors of the Uruguayan plane crash had to consume the bodies of
their dead companions. There were only six
corpses that remained untouched: three females
and three males."

During the rescue operation carried out by three volunteers of the Andean Rescue Corps and an Army medical corporal, they learned the dramatic details of the epic struggle for survival in the high sierras.

After descending from the helicopter, the rescue team saw something they had never seen before, in spite of their long experience with all kinds of strange events. The squadron chief, Claudio Lucero, stepped on a woman's hand which protruded from the snow, with painted fingernails and part of the palm and forearm torn away. He saw dismembered limbs, pieces of skulls and other parts of the human body. And when he approached the presumed leader of the group, he was treated with a certain aloofness, consequently having to assert his authority to convince him that they had come to rescue them, to help them.

Then, as they were approaching the fuselage, Lucero picked up a skull and asked the young men, "Whose skull is this?" And the leader answered, "It belonged to the pilot." They had eaten his brains, but spared his body, which is still in the pilot's cabin.

He said: "Our hunger and desperation got much worse when we heard on the radio that they were abandoning the search."

As the food became scarcer day by day, Roberto Canessa, a medical student, started convincing them that they would have to eat the bodies of their dead companions to stay alive. He explained that their flesh contained proteins, which the survivors would need to survive in the isolated cordillera. One of them wanted to commit suicide with a gun, but Canessa wouldn't let him. With razor blades that he kept in a box, the medical student sliced the principal parts of the body and made a daily distribution of minimal rations.

"God helped us," they said. "When the avalanche came and killed several more people, five of the bodies were buried in the snow, which served as a refrigerator. The other bodies were taken elsewhere."

From the rafters inside the fuselage they had hung the dismembered arms and legs to distill the bodily oils, which the rescue squad themselves noticed when they entered the cabin to prepare some soup. And the stench was unbearable.

The crippled plane is precariously slanted at a 60-degree angle, and at any moment it could easily slide into the bottom of the deep canyon.

During the last night the survivors spent in their makeshift dormitory, Sergio Diaz, one of the rescuers, encouraged them to sing a few songs and to recite some poetry, entertaining them as much as possible for a few hours, trying to bolster their spirits and convincing them their terrible ordeal was over.

But for his own purposes, he placed his tent outside the cabin, so that he might help save the Uruguayans if the fuselage should suddenly slide into the canyon. He spent most of the following morning outside the fuselage gathering the skulls and dismembered limbs and trying to rejoin them with the bodies, which were then tagged with identification markers, assuming they might later be picked up for burial elsewhere. Meanwhile, his fellow alpinists and the survivors searched all around for their dead companions' personal property, so that it could be turned over to their parents. In one suitcase they found a camera, jewels, a watch and money.

During one of their long conversations, the survivors told Sergio Diaz that in choosing a leader, they had applied the law of the jungle: The strongest man ruled. . . .

While the *La Segunda* reporters were writing their sensational revelations, Fernando Parrado dropped by the photo department in search of various pictures showing the damaged fuselage, the rescue at Los Maitenes, their arrival in Santiago, and also the Hotel Sheraton, where most of the survivors were staying.

The correspondents approached Parrado and asked to interview him about various news stories and official statements regarding the alleged consumption of human flesh during their long isolation in the Andes.

La Segunda asked: "Certain daily newspapers have quoted various sources, including a young woman who says that her fiance had told her some horrifying things which implied that you'd eaten human flesh in order to survive. Any comment?"

Parrado answered: "No one has said anything about that. That's totally unfounded. Those statements have no basis. No one has said any such thing."

When the reporter pressed him for further remarks on the published articles, Parrado added, "I'm only saying that no one has said anything."

But the reporter persisted: "The news media quote a report by the *Cuerpo de Socorro Andino* which states that upon entering the fuselage its three members had seen desiccated human limbs hanging from the ceiling and that inside the cabin there was an odor of putrefaction."

"Whatever that report says—if it's reported by responsible people—they ought to know what they're doing," said Parrado.

"Do you know about that report—and have you read it?"

"No, I know nothing about it. I haven't read any report. There is nothing official. The newspapers have invented an awful lot."

"The newspapers say that none of you were emaciated after remaining seventy-two days in the very heart of the cordillera, without food and in freezing temperatures—that upon your arrival in Santiago you seemed to be in good shape even though considerably underweight, and that this was due to your consumption of human flesh. What have you to say about that?"

Fingering the buttons on his blue shirt, which hung

loosely on his bony shoulders and arms, Parrado smiled. "We've all lost a lot of weight. I lost fifty or sixty pounds. We were all quite strong. Bear in mind that we're rugby players. I weighed about 200 or 205 pounds and measured about six feet in height. Now I weigh less than 155 pounds. If you had seen me before the accident, you'd be frightened seeing me now. Anyway, all that has been said about eating human flesh is unfounded. There is nothing official. We're beginning to think that the press is speculating about other aspects of our ordeal in order to stir up more interest."

Finally, the reporter pressed him for an outright confirmation or denial of statements by his companions or those cited in the report of the Andean Rescue Corps; but Parrado was adamant. "I don't deny or confirm anything. Those reports are not official. They're merely hearsay."

Then he said that he was leaving soon for a few more days rest at Vina del Mar, returning on Saturday for an afternoon flight to Montevideo. "We'll go by plane," he said, grinning and touching his chapped and still infected lower lip. "I don't think I'll have a second accident. Anyway, I now have much more experience in such matters." Then, accompanied by his brother-in-law, he bid everyone farewell and asked *La Segunda* to thank the many Chileans who had been so kind and understanding.

Referring again to various news stories just before he left, Parrado said, "The newspaper that has been the most accurate in reporting what happened in the cordillera is *El Mercurio*. Others have fabricated statements attributed to us—and even a phony press release."

When offered a cigarette by one of the staff members, he said he never smoked, then added that "Some of my friends smoked like fiends. We had found a huge amount of cigarettes in the tail section of the plane, and they smoked every one, along with eating all the chocolate and bonbons that we bought in Mendoza."

An hour later, Roberto Canessa was interviewed by

La Segunda, and he seemed less evasive than Parrado—but still not entirely candid. "We found some dry herbs and other plants—but, as a student of medicine, I knew they had no proteins—and that's what we needed to stay alive."

Since he was accompanied by his fiancee, the reporters failed to hound him for a specific answer, nevertheless assuming that "he was implicitly confirming what people are saying in hushed voices: that the survivors of the accident had to eat human flesh in order to survive."

Later on, however, one of the more obstinate newsmen bluntly asked Canessa if he had any comments on the Rescue Corps report to Air Force authorities, and the usually soft-spoken youth responded with a hint of anger: "Regarding that report and the morbid details about what was seen inside the cabin, my position is very clear. If there are people who are interested in that sort of thing, such people are of no concern to me. I might respect someone who feeds his curiosity with such things, but I certainly can't like him."

Refusing any further discussion of the controversial issue, Canessa explained that "we've made an agreement among ourselves not to talk about this particular matter. Nothing relating to what we ate. Why pursue such morbid details? There are other matters to talk about. Why can't we discuss, for example, how we watched our dearest friends dying, their eyes staring blankly at the sky as they pleaded for help, while we stood by unable to save them or to relieve their suffering—why not talk about that? It's easy to hear or to read about such things—but we had to live through them, and there's a big difference."

Canessa would occasionally look at Laura, who seemed as emotionally strong as he was. When someone mentioned the nightmare they had experienced and how it might effect the mental stability of the survivors, Roberto shook his head. "They're okay. I'm sure they won't be affected by what has happened. They're just a little tired and physically weak. That's all."

"But, Roberto," interjected Laura. "Some of them are very emotionally upset."

"No, no," he quickly replied. "They're just exhausted. They'll recover eventually. Because we had this great unity, this fantastic spirit among us. Those of us who went out in search of help weren't relying just on our own spiritual strength—it was our total solidarity that inspired us, that gave us the courage to leave the plane and risk the unknown.

"But regarding the food we ate to stay alive, I can say no more. We've made an agreement that we've got to keep."

At the bottom of the above-translated news story, *La Segunda* published an angry disclaimer by the director of the *Cuerpo de Soccoro Andino:* "None of the participants in the rescue of the survivors has made any statements—official or personal—to the press about alleged acts of cannibalism at the site of the accident. With respect to certain published reports about such statements, Sergio Diaz, Claudio Lucero, and Osvaldo Villegas deny having made any statements at any time to the news media. They have indignantly denounced such reports and characterize them as a prejudicial campaign against Chile and the agencies that participated in the rescue."

The commander of the Air Force Rescue Service, Juan Ivanovic, who coordinated the joint rescue operations, also emphatically denied that any reports had been issued to the press. And in a separate interview, the highly incensed members of the Andean Rescue Corps further reiterated that it is not uncommon to find dismembered human limbs around a plane that has crashed. This official denial was delivered to the press in Santiago at 1:30 P.M., after an emergency meeting between officials of the Andean Rescue Corps, and the Air Force Minister of Interior.

Later that afternoon, the same three agencies issued separate formal statements that must have confused the general public even further. The Air Force, speaking through its director of public relations, Patricio Araya

Ugalde, once again disclaimed any involvement in the published reports: "There never was, nor is there now, any confidential report issued by the Air Force Resue Service, and any reference to this alleged document lacks veracity."

The Secretaria General de Gobierno, represented by Deputy Minister Arsenio Poupin, issued a carefully worded statement clearly reflecting the President's concern about possible international repercussions.

But the Andean Rescue Corps, a volunteer, non-governmental organization, wittingly or unwittingly tantalized the press with a formal statement that was bound to encourage the kind of speculation the government had deplored. After the customary repetitive and stilted preface, the Rescue Corps declared that "the rescue squad, having been transported by helicopters, remained at the site with the eight survivors for two days. Thereafter, the pertinent authorities were informed that dismembered and desiccated remains of human bodies were scattered around the fuselage, and that further details had been provided by the survivors themselves. This information was subsequently relayed to Cesar Charlone, Charge d'Affaires for the Uruguayan embassy, by the director of the Andean Rescue Corps, Guillerma Silva, and by Juan Gabriel Bustos, head of public relations. It was agreed at said time that the Andean Rescue Corps would conduct a Christian burial for the deceased."

Reporters for rival newspapers, who had been scooped by *La Segunda,* were quick to note that the Andean Rescue Corps' unpaid publicist, Juan Bustos, was also managing editor of *El Mercurio,* the principal newspaper of the chain that also owns *La Segunda,* which explains why both dailies had ready access to the supposedly confidential official report. Moreover, *El Mercurio,* in its next edition, published an enlarged photograph on the front page, showing a macabre collection of mangled legs and arms half-buried in the snow near the plane's battered nose. *La Segunda* published a similar but much smaller photograph in which the grisly details were obscured in dark ink. Both photos were presumably obtained from the Rescue Corps or from one of its three-man rescue team.

Meanwhile, in faraway Montevideo, where local newspapers were still maintaining a respectful silence on the issue of cannibalism, an Associated Press reporter had telephoned the home of one of the survivors, Roberto Francois; and when his mother, who took the call, was asked to comment on reports publicized in Chile, she angrily denied everything.

"That's a lie!" she snapped. "And I think it's criminal for anyone to publish such vile rumors. That's incredible. That couldn't have happened among these boys. After all, they got strict moral training at the Colegio Stella Maris, and a profound Christian faith."

Refusing to let anyone interview her son, Mrs. Sara Francois asked the reporter, "Can you imagine the horrible pain such a rumor will cause him?"

When the same correspondent tried to talk with Daniel Fernandez, who had also returned to Montevideo, he would neither confirm nor deny the notorious reports. "I prefer not to talk about it," was all he would say. "It's very disturbing."

Thousands of parents in Santiago were also shocked and indignant—but for a different reason. Their children, especially the younger ones, were having violent reactions to the lurid, gruesome photographs and news stories prominent in the press and on television and radio stations. Hundreds of irate mothers were contacting editorial offices to complain that their children were having horrifying nightmares, refusing to eat, or immediately vomiting when they did. On the other hand, many youngsters were morbidly fascinated and were literally driving their parents to distraction by refusing to talk about anything else.

"Mama, what's anthropophagy?" Juan would teasingly ask, having just been told for the tenth time by another brother or sister (or father) that it was a less revolting way of saying "cannibalism."

From the very outset, some newspapers avoided saying *canibalismo,* preferring the seemingly more delicate and abstract term, *antropofagia.* But the more sensationalist tabloids gave vent to a verbalistic orgy, using headlines like: "MACABRE MENU! . . . WE FED ON DEATH. . . . JUSTIFIED CANNIBALISM."

"Those editors are pigs who don't deserve to live," sobbed the mother of Carlos Paez, holding a crumpled and torn copy of *La Segunda.* "These stories are grotesque. All they want is to sell more papers. They don't care about human dignity, nor about the horrible pain my son and his companions have suffered."

Displayed side-by-side on newsstands throughout Santiago, rival newspapers seemed to snarl and snap at each other like angry dogs fighting over a juicy bone, but the reporters themselves (with few exceptions) were much less belligerent as they swarmed through the lobby, cocktail lounges, dining rooms, and outside terraces of the Sheraton Hotel. Hoping to interview or at least catch a glimpses of the survivors if they should suddenly leave their rooms, some of the competing journalists casually bought drinks for each other as they waited in the downstairs bar.

"I thought you guys were enemies," said one of the waiters, smilingly pointing at the bitterly accusatory headlines on two newspapers someone had left on their table.

"That's part of the game, Miguel," one of them answered, winking at his colleagues. "That's what sells newspapers—lots of controversy."

"Claro," another one added. "If we all agreed, *che,* the public would be bored."

Seven floors above them, in a large, well-furnished room, one of the sixteen victims of the headline competition was staring out the window, a hint of tears in his puffed, red-veined eyes. As his mother tried to console him, he could hear the muffled voices of pretty bikini-clad bathers around the turquoise swimming pool, where he himself had lain in the sun surrounded by admiring *senoritas.* But he wouldn't be seeing them today—nor the day after. Having secluded himself in his room to escape prying reporters, he had refused to eat anything since the first news stories about cannibalism had appeared. The wastebasket near his bed was brimming over with various newspapers which he had insisted on reading despite tearful pleas from his parents to ignore them.

"We should have admitted it right away," he told his father. "We wanted to tell everyone. We didn't want to hide it. But people kept advising us not to talk about it. And now look what's happening. They're crucifying us. As if we we were trying to conceal something awful. . . ."

The youthful survivor in the room down the hall was far less voluble. With his parents sitting quietly near the window, he lay on the bed, blankly staring at the ceiling, refusing to eat or even to talk. Fingering a rosary of smooth ebony beads, the filigreed silver crucifix dangled on her lap, his distraught mother whispered to her husband that during lunch someone had mentioned a statement by an official at the Vatican.

She was referring to an editorial in *L'Osservatore Romano,* official organ of the Holy See, which unequivocally affirmed: "One cannot speak of cannibalism in the case of the young Uruguayans who survived in the Andes, particularly if one presumes they had to nourish themselves with the remains of the deceased in order to survive." Subsequently, cables from Vatican news services quoted a more complete statement by an authoritative theologian, Father Dino Concetti, presumably reflecting the views of the Pope himself:

"The dramatic episode experienced by survivors of the Uruguayan Air Force plane crash cannot, under any circumstances, be classified as cannibalism. If one assumes that an organ from a dead body may be justifiably transplanted into the body of a living human being, then—in a case of extreme necessity—why should it not be justified for these men to use the entire body in order to survive? Their action merely bears a resemblance to cannibalism. But the need to survive eliminates any negative aspect from their conduct. If the circumstances veritably evolved as most reports indicate, this unhappy occurrence cannot from a theological viewpoint be considered an act of cannibalism. The Catholic Church commands respect for the dead, and does so on the basis of profound theological reasons. All deceased bodies have been inhabited by a Soul, and with that Soul they have participated in human life. But after death, the Soul leaves the body, which is then destined to inevitable decomposition. Consequently, with such principles taken into account, it was ethically justifiable for the survivors to consume the cadavers of their companions so as to stay alive. Moreover, as all evidence indicates, they had no other available source of food."

Analyzing the problem from a nontheological point of view, Dr. Miguel Schweitzer, professor of criminal law at the University of Chile, provided an additional ounce of comfort with the following legal opinion, typically couched in those contingent phrases so favored by lawyers: "Assuming the accuracy of published reports concerning the anthropophagy practiced by the sixteen survivors of the said accident, such acts, according to Chilean law, are exempt from culpability and not susceptible to legal responsibility since they were acting in a state of extreme duress. One must presume they were motivated by an irresistible impulse, or that they had no other viable recourse."

Of more direct practical significance were the psychiatric observations of a professor of medicine at the same university: "In certain situations of extreme terror, hunger, great danger, or death itself, there may be cases which psychiatrists describe as 'a darkening of the conscience' or 'psychic blindness.' In such mental states there occurs an abeyance of suspicion, decency, repugnance, shame, and other ethical restraints. Lucidity is not sufficient for a sense of moral responsibility. But the danger of serious emotional conflicts is always present when a person emerges from that psychic blindness and becomes genuinely aware of what he has done during that period of blurred conscience."

Understandably fearing the impact of such statements if the already distraught survivors should read or hear them on the radio (there were no television sets in their rooms), their parents hurriedly made plans to leave Santiago on the following day. "This city has become a living hell for them," one of them remarked. "We've got to get back to Montevideo."

Meanwhile, the embattled Charge d'Affaires of the Uruguayan embassy, Cesar Charlone, had been summoned home by an irate Minister of Foreign Affairs. Before leaving Chile he had told reporters, "This was indeed a miracle, and no one can minimize in any way the indisputable fact that these sixteen youngsters were protagonists in the grandest feat in history. I won't accept cheap sensationalism about what has happened— and I shall be at their side to confront that kind of yellow journalism." Having heard that challenging statement on radio stations in Montevideo, scores of reporters (who had flown beforehand to Uruguay to meet the survivors on their arrival), were waiting to meet Charlone when his plane came in at 5:20 P.M. on December 27. They were expecting him to clarify conflicting versions of what had been happening in Chile, and, more particularly, were eager to ask what role he had played in releasing the much disputed "confidential official report" which the Andean Rescue Corps had allegedly given him.

But Charlone refused to answer any questions. Recalling how accessible he had been to the press in San Fernando and Santiago, the reporters chased after him from one section of the airport to another. "I can't say anything, I can't say anything," he kept mumbling as he pushed through them in a desperate search for help from the protocol officer he had assumed would meet him. Sweating profusely and clenching his hands, he suddenly bolted out of the waiting room toward the parking lot. But just outside the building a group of older men and women (later identified as parents of the deceased passengers) blocked his way and began insulting him, accusing him of a callous attitude during the first few weeks after the accident.

"You told us not to bother you anymore!" one of them yelled. "You didn't give a damn."

"You kept telling us to wait until the spring thaw and to leave you alone."

"And when we asked you to get us a car so we could drive to the mountains to look for the plane ourselves, you ignored us, you turned your back on us!"

"You wouldn't even help us arrange for an exemption on currency exchanges—it was too much work for you!"

"And when you refused to meet with us, we had to make our own arrangements with the Chilean government—without any help from you, *because it was your siesta hour.*"

"You wouldn't lift a finger for our boys—and now you're trying to play the big hero, you lousy hypocrite!"

Nonplussed by their rage and tearful frustration, Charlone simply stood mute, his eyes averted, his arms hanging limp. "I have no comment," he finally said, backing away from them. "I can't say anything now. I have to go."

Half stumbling and then running frantically, he raced toward the parking lot, with several reporters in pursuit. But when he got inside a parked car, he suddenly realized it wasn't his and scrambled out again. Pinned between two other vehicles, his lips trembling, he begged the newsmen to leave him alone. "I've got to talk with the Minister first. And I can't say anything before that. Please understand—I simply can't talk."

Two hours later, as he was leaving the Chancery of the Palacio Santos, Charlone held a short, impromptu press conference for the few correspondents who had stuck with him. "I wasn't able to answer your questions at the airport because of my prior engagement with the Minister. While on the plane, a special envoy from the foreign office informed me that I was not to make any further statements to the press until after our meeting. Dr. Blanco has asked me to obtain an exact word-for-word text of what I said in Chile. And, accordingly, it will be reviewed by the Minister at his convenience."

He also announced that the survivors would arrive in Montevideo on the following afternoon, and would hold a press conference in the auditorium of El Colegio Stella Maris. "They have chosen to delay any comments on this tragic event until they can do so in Uruguay and among Uruguayans. So you shall finally hear the whole truth from those who really know it."

X

Psychic Trauma—Black Humor

"Let's suppose for the sake of argument, Pepe, that they had actually killed some of their companions in order to procure the food necessary to survive—would you still say they were justified?"

Such questions were the focus of thousands of conversations all over Chile—on street corners, in hotel lobbies, barbershops, bars, restaurants, book stores, offices, park benches, and wherever two or more people congregated—but this particular query was posed during a pre-dinner cocktail hour at the home of Pepe and Alice Stevenson in a mountainside suburb of Santiago. Among their guests was Dr. Cesar Cecchi, a well-known pediatrician, professor of architecture, music and art critic, translator into Spanish of French and American plays, and gifted raconteur—a Renaissance man, in every sense of the word. Dr. Cecchi is also a long-time friend and confidant of President Salvador Allende and his brilliant wife, a most happy circumstance which subsequently enabled this writer to interview various doctors and government officials who had

had close and extended contacts with the sixteen survivors.

Having heard that the young Uruguayans would be holding a press conference on their arrival in Montevideo the next day, the irrepressibly speculative doctor could barely wait to quiz his hosts on what he considered "the ultimate extension" of the moral dilemma everyone had been discussing. Thus, even before taking his first sip of sherry, he asked the opening question: "Let's suppose for the sake of argument, Pepe, that they had actually killed some of their companions in order to procure the food necessary to survive—would you still say they were justified?"

Leaning back in his favorite chair, his elbow resting on one of the lower shelves of a floor-to-ceiling bookcase, Pepe pursed his lips and drew a deep sigh. "Yes," he finally said. "I do think they would have been justified to go to that extreme."

"But, why?" asked his nineteen-year-old daughter Francisca, generally known as Panchi.

"Well, first of all, I'm not a lawyer, nor a theologian —just a humble engineer who now and then delves into other matters—but I can easily imagine a group of men so emotionally unbalanced by incipient starvation and death, so completely deranged, if only temporarily, that they would have to be considered exempt from the usual rules of human conduct."

"I would certainly agree," said Dr. Cecchi. "And there's considerable medical and psychiatric literature that would support your view."

"And you may have some legal support," I said, referring to "The Case of the Speluncean Explorers," a mythical court decision written for the *Harvard Law Review* by Professor Lon L. Fuller in 1949. "One of my more inventive law professors projected his imaginary case to the year 4299, and the defendants were a group of explorers who had been imprisoned in a cave when a landslide covered its only opening. A rescue party was immediately sent to the cave, but soon realized it would probably take at least a month to get them out. Since it was known that the five explorers had carried only minimal provisions, and since it was also known that there was no animal or vegetable matter within the cave, it was generally feared the men would starve to death before anyone could save them. Fortunately, they had a radio transmitter-receiver, and within a few days they asked to speak with a doctor about their fear of starvation, ultimately asking him if they would be able to survive ten more days by eating the flesh of one of their group. Later on, the apparent leader [Roger Whetmore] asked the same doctor if it would be advisable for them to cast lots to determine which of them should be eaten. And when he refused to give an opinion, Whetmore asked for advice from a lawyer, a government official, and a minister or a priest —none of whom would offer any comment on the matter."

"Now, there was a real dilemma," said Alice, vaguely recalling that a law student had told her about the case while she was at Radcliffe College. "But I don't quite remember what action they took. Except that it was pretty gruesome."

"Quite gruesome," I said, accepting another Scotch from Pepe before proceeding with Professor Fuller's tale. "They eventually drew lots and Whetmore lost, even though he had backed out of the lottery before the actual drawing."

"And they killed him anyway?" asked Panchi, frowning as if the event had actually occurred.

"They certainly did," I said. "Killed him and ate him. And that's what gave rise to the murder trial, the conviction, and the subsequent appeal to the Supreme Court of the mythical Commonwealth of Newgarth."

"And what was the decision?" asked one of Panchi's university classmates.

"Well, the court was evenly divided, so the conviction was upheld and the defendants finally executed in the year 4300 A.D."

"That's stupid," said Pepe, temporarily forgetting that the case wouldn't take place for another 2,328 years. "How could they possibly say they were murderers?"

Taking a copy of Fuller's article from my briefcase, I turned to the sixth page and told Pepe, "Here's one justice who totally agrees with your reasoning. Just listen to this:

> . . . Now I contend that a case may be removed morally from the force of a legal order, as well as geographically. If we look to the purposes of law and government, and to the premises underlying our positive law, these men when they made their fateful decision were as remote from our legal order as if they had been a thousand miles beyond our boundaries. . . .
>
> I conclude, therefore, that at the time Roger Whetmore's life was ended by these defendants, they were, to use the quaint language of the nineteenth-century writers, not in a 'state of civil society' but in a 'state of nature.' This has the consequence that the law applicable to them is not the enacted and established law of this Commonwealth. . . ."

"Now there's a wise and just man," said Pepe, lighting his pipe and fanning the match long after it was extinguished. "And those same principles, both of morality and law, would certainly apply to the much less serious case of the sixteen survivors of the air crash. They're guilty of nothing—not a damned thing, as far as I'm concerned."

"I agree," said Cesar. "But do you think *they* feel guiltless?"

"That's a very good question," said Alice, running her hand across the middle shelf of the bookcase. "But before we get into that, Cesar, I'd like to find out if cannibal pioneers in the famous Donner case were ever tried for murder. There's a book about it somewhere on this shelf."

"It's out near the pool," said Pepe, "I was leafing

through it just before Cesar and Hank arrived. The book is called *The Donner Party,* and it's a long narrative poem, which sort of surprised me. I had expected an historical novel."

"Do you mean it's a poem about cannibalism?" asked Panchi. "That's an awfully strange theme for poetry."

"It wasn't only cannibalism, Panchi," said Pepe. "Those American pioneers actually killed some of their companions and then ate them. So it was different from this Uruguayan incident—more like that mythical Speluncean case Hank was talking about. Either way, they were justified. But I guess you'd have to say that the rugby players were less guilty."

"Well, that leads me back to my previous question," said Cesar. "Do you really think these young Uruguayans feel guiltless, Pepe, even though most of us outsiders agree that they're blameless?"

"I'm afraid not," said Pepe. "Especially when you consider that one of them—I think his name was Turcatti—refused to eat human flesh and deliberately starved himself to death."

"And that's precisely why their team doctor also urged them to convince everybody—to get unanimous consent," said Cesar. "That doctor knew that unanimity, complete agreement, was a psychological necessity."

"But why?" someone asked.

"Because they were violating one of the most ancient of taboos, and a failure to get unanimous agreement would inevitably leave a residue of guilt among all the others," answered Cesar. "Freud mentions this in a marvelous book he wrote called *Totem and Taboo.*"

"There's a copy of it on the shelf near your elbow," said Alice, motioning to Pepe. "It has a blue cover. If I'm not mistaken, I've underlined the passage."

"Good," said Cesar. "Let me read it to Panchi and Hank."

Quickly riffling the pages as if he might be able to recognize the desired paragraph in a split second (which he apparently did), Cesar sat back in his chair and started reading:

" 'There is not the least doubt that every sacrifice was originally a clan sacrifice, and that the *killing of a sacrificial animal* originally belonged to those acts which were *forbidden to the individual and were only justified if the whole kin assumed the responsibility*. Primitive men'—and here you've got to bear in mind that these Uruguayan survivors were temporarily back in a 'state of nature,' as Professor Fuller's judge characterized the cave explorers. Anyway, 'primitive men had only one class of actions which were thus characterized, namely, actions which touched the holiness of the kin's common blood. A life which no individual might take and which could be sacrificed *only through the consent and participation of all the members of the clan* was on the same plane as the life of a member of the kin. *The rule that every guest of the sacrificial repast must partake of the flesh of the sacrificial animal had the same meaning as the rule that the execution of a guilty member of the kin must be performed by the whole kin.*' "

"But that refers mostly to killing," said Panchi. "There was no killing among the Uruguayans."

"Nevertheless, the same principle of unanimous consent applies to this case, because they, too, have violated a taboo."

"Cesar's right," said Alice. "And there's another passage in *Totem and Taboo* that expands on his point. It's right on the next page: 'We have heard that in later times every eating in common, the participation in the same substance which entered into their bodies, established a holy bond between the communicants. . . . Such an idea was the basis of all the *blood bonds* through which men in still later times became pledged to each other. . . .' And here's a kind of summary of what Freud was getting at. 'There is also the conscious realization that an action is being carried out which is forbidden to each individual and which can only be justified through the participation of all, so that no one is allowed to exclude himself from the killing *and the feast*.' "

Cesar nodded slowly as he referred once again to Dr. Nicola. "As we said, that's what he advised Canessa and Parrado just before he died—that they should try to get unanimous agreement to eat the flesh of their dead companions. And then Turcatti refused. Oh, he agreed to go along, all right—though not really. He just couldn't. But I'm afraid his refusal to eat, his decision to die instead, will haunt those kids for a long time. For Turcatti was actually the collective conscience of all of them, the conscience that refused to enter that so-called 'state of nature.' "

"But wasn't Turcatti's action a form of suicide?" asked Alice, fingering the stem of her slender wine glass. "And wouldn't that be a mortal sin, according to Catholic dogma?"

"Not really," said Pepe. "Because, after all, suicide is an affirmative act, or you might more accurately call it an affirmative negative act. But whatever you call it, Alice, it's not the passive kind of thing that Turcatti did. He didn't *kill* himself: He merely let himself die. And there's a big difference between the two—at least to my way of thinking."

Alice smiled in agreement, "Okay, I'll accept that—but there's one other thing I'd like to ask all of you: Do you think Turcatti was refusing out of principle and moral scruple—or was he merely being squeamish and cat-picky?"

"Now that's a wonderful phrase," I said, jotting it down. "Cat-picky, cat-picky. I'll have to quote you, Alice."

"Never mind quoting me—just answer my question. Any of you."

"It was probably squeamishness," said Pepe. "He just couldn't stomach the idea of eating human flesh—for esthetic reasons. Especially since it was raw. I myself might have hesitated to eat it for that reason alone—but not on account of any moral scruples."

Cesar grinned and sipped his sherry before commenting. "But what if it were cooked, Pepe?"

"I'd have no problem then; and perhaps Turcatti

could have changed *his* mind if the meat had been cooked."

"Why didn't they cook it?"

"Because they had no fuel, Panchi. None at all. They had to eat it raw. That's why they sliced it into awfully small pieces and made them into pellets."

"How did you find out that, Cesar?"

"One of the doctors told me. I guess the survivors admitted just about everything to him. They didn't hold back on anything. They really had a healthy psychological impulse to confess everything from the very beginning, but everyone—including all the doctors they saw —kept advising them not to talk about it."

"That must have confused hell out of them."

"Of course it did, and undoubtedly made them feel the guilt they weren't supposed to feel. After all, when you tell someone to conceal or deny something he's done, he's bound to think there's something pretty awful about it."

"And they couldn't have kept it secret anyway," said Alice. "People were bound to find out—especially the reporters."

"They could have been kinder," observed Panchi. "Those headlines were awful. And I was surprised to see how *La Segunda* and *El Mercurio* dealt with them."

"Why were you surprised?"

"Because they're conservative newspapers, always defending the middle and upper classes; and, after all, the Uruguayans are mostly upper-class kids—nephews of the President of Uruguay, sons of wealthy doctors, lawyers, and businessmen. So you'd think they would have done a little cover-up instead of blasting the front pages with all this stuff about cannibalism."

"That brings up another point," said Pepe, pouring himself more sherry. "How do you think a bunch of poor guys—how would they have acted in this situation?"

"Well, first of all," said Cesar, "I don't think they would have eaten human flesh."

"Why not?"

"Because people in the poorer classes tend to be more superstitious than those from the wealthier, more educated groups. And as you know, some of them would think that eating human flesh would cause them to become like the devil—that they would be cursed forever. Or they might feel like vampires."

"That may be true," added Panchi. "But don't you also think that a group of poorer, less educated people might have acted more savagely if they'd got to the point of insanity as a result of starvation? Because that's what happened with the pioneers in the Donner Party; they went mad with hunger."

"Possibly," said Cesar. "But anyone—rich or poor —might eventually go mad with hunger. Except that in this particular case there were some medical students and a dying doctor who devised some fairly sophisticated ways of making their anthropophagy slightly less odious. In other words, they weren't chomping hunks of flesh off the bone itself, with blood dripping from their mouths. So, in that sense, I guess you might say that an upper-class education helped them figure out ways to make some things less revolting. They were more genteel, let's say."

"That reminds me of a book about some people who were the very opposite of genteel or gentle," said Alice. "It's called *The Mountain People,* by Colin Turnbull."

"The one about the Iks?"

"That's right, Panchi. We were talking about them the other day when *La Segunda* published its first story about cannibalism in the cordillera."

"What about the Iks?" I asked.

"Well, they're supposed to be awfully cruel with each other—with members of their own family. They live in a very poverty-stricken area of northern Uganda, where food is very scarce, and they'll sometimes take food away from their own parents—if they're too old and sick to defend themselves—and simply let them starve to death. And they've even been known to let their own children do the same. It's every man for himself and to hell with anyone else. But—and here's the eally surprising thing—*they never engage in cannibal-ism,* as far as anyone knows. That's strictly taboo, no matter how mean, cruel, or degenerate they are in other ways."

"That's strange," said Pepe. "But it sort of supports what Cesar was saying about the greater amount of superstition and taboos among the less educated and the poor."

"But the rich and the poor are equally sexist," said Panchi with an impish gleam in her eyes.

"Now how does *sexism* come into the picture?" asked her father.

"I was thinking about the Uruguayan survivors and their *macho* decision to spare the ladies' bodies—or, if worse came to worst, to eat them last. Now, that's pure sexism!"

There was a burst of laughter, which she obviously expected; but she persisted. "It *was* sexist, when you really analyze it. I can just see them proudly patting themselves on the back for gallantly deciding to spare the female corpses until the very end. Now, don't you think that was kind of ridiculous and phony?"

"Umm—I'm not so sure, Panchi," said Alice. "I think it was kind of sweet and old-fashioned."

"Would *you* rather be eaten first?" asked Pepe.

"It wouldn't make any difference if I were dead," said Panchi. "But it just seems silly and incongruous to make that phony distinction between men and women when you're dealing with cannibalism."

"Maybe you're right," said Cesar. "But why do you keep calling it cannibalism?"

"Because that's what it was. They ate human flesh, and that's cannibalism."

"Not exactly, Panchi. When you kill in order to eat human flesh, that's *canibalismo;* but when you merely eat the flesh of someone who's already dead, that's *antropofagia.*"

Recalling that Cesar, as well as most Chilean editorial writers, had been insisting on discriminating between the words "cannibalism" and "anthropophagy," I asked him if the Spanish dictionaries made that distinction, which doesn't appear in the American dictionaries I've checked—all of which equate one word with the other.

"I'm sure ours does," said Cesar. "At least the dictionary of the Spanish Academy. But I've frankly never looked it up."

"We'll do it right now," said Pepe, reaching for a thick book on the shelf behind him. "I've been making the same distinction as Cesar. . . . But I'm afraid we're wrong. There is no such difference as far as the dictionary goes."

Cesar smiled and nodded his head. "That just goes to show how some words build up negative connotations, while others remain neutral. I guess the word *antropofagia* sounds less repulsive, so we've used it to make a distinction we needed to make."

"It's also easier to swallow," said Alice. "If you'll excuse a rather sick pun."

"That's not half as sick as some of the black humor that's popped up since the cannibal story appeared," said Panchi.

"Such as?"

"Well, the latest one has to do with the survivors at that special Christmas mass, where Monsignor Hasbun gave them communion—so the big question going all over town is: Why does Monsignor Hasbun have only three fingers?"

Laughter and someone saying, "That's really sick," then a joke from Cesar. "This is the one about the stewardess on the plane which the survivors are reluctantly riding back to Montevideo. When she gives the luncheon menu to one of the Uruguayans, he says, 'Never mind the menu—just give me the passenger list.'"

"But the sickest joke of all," said Pepe, "is the one about. . . ."

(It was indeed the sickest and the most fiendishly humorous of the many jokes floating around Santiago and Montevideo, but I have decided to spare the sensibilities of the reader and my editors by omitting it.)*

As one story led to another, Cesar was reminded of his ten-year-old niece's reaction to an anecdote based on a semantic twist on the word *antropofagia*. Joining in the adults' laughter, she had doubled over with glee, as if she had really understood the punch line; but when she subsequently learned what the word actually meant, she rushed into the bathroom to vomit and thereafter refused to eat dinner.

"It was a fairly innocuous story," said Cesar, "much milder than the ones the survivors must have invented about themselves."

"Do you really think they made jokes about their own cannibalism?"

"Of course. That's the basis of all black or gallows humor," answered Cesar. "Whenever people get into a tragic situation—whether they're in the 'death row' of a prison, in the military trenches, in cancer wards, or marooned and abandoned after an accident—they somehow relieve their tension and despair by joking about themselves. Some of the most bitter, most poignant humor I've ever heard was stories Jews invented about their suffering during the pogroms in Poland and Hitler's Germany. So I'm almost certain these young Uruguayans created quite a bit of 'sick' humor about their own 'cannibalism.' Otherwise, they wouldn't have been able to suppress the guilt and revulsion they must have felt when they broke that ancient taboo."

"What now, Cesar? Will they be able to shake off the psychic trauma?"

"I sure hope so, Pepe. But it's going to be a long haul. It would have been so much easier if they had followed their original impulse to talk freely about it. After all, Pepe, they could have buried all those dismembered limbs that were scattered around the fuselage, and got rid of the meat hanging inside the cabin. They'd heard on their radio that the rescue helicopter

---

* The editors insisted on hearing the story and readily agreed with the author's decision to exclude it.

was on the way, so they had plenty of time to dispose of the evidence. Quite obviously, they wanted everyone to know. And, psychologically speaking, that was a healthy impulse. But then everyone began to confuse them, to stir up feelings of guilt. Obeying those father figures, the doctors and priests—and in their fragile psychic state, they were in desperate need of surrogate fathers—they've been trying to conceal what everyone knew or had guessed. And it's painful to see them inventing explanations which they obviously know are ridiculous. Consequently, every hour of this clumsy, futile deception merely compounds the guilt they shouldn't be feeling."

"I totally agree," said Alice, with a sudden sadness. "But what will they say tomorrow, Cesar, when they get back to Montevideo for the press conference? What explanations will they give?"

"Who can possibly guess, Alice? I certainly can't. But I hope they'll come up with some rationale that will make all this horror they've been through—this journalistic trauma—just a bit more bearable. Because when all the public furor dies down, each one of those young men will be facing a terribly lonely reexamination of himself."

"And there's one other problem," said Pepe. "Something quite apart from the psychological aftermath of cannibalism—"

"Which is?"

"I'm thinking of the problem which some psychologists call *survival guilt*," he continued. "For some people, apparently, there's an enormous burden of guilt that arises from the mere fact of survival in circumstances where many others have died—wars, earthquakes, floods, fires, shipwrecks, plane crashes. 'Why wasn't *I* killed?' they'll ask. I've heard that many Jews who survived the concentration camps have never got rid of the guilt they feel because they got out and their mothers, fathers, sisters, brothers, and dearest friends died in the ovens."

"That's right," said Alice. "And there's an added

element to that guilt: Those who survive often feel that they owe something to someone, and it's a debt that can't ever be paid. So it's a perpetual nagging burden."

"That's so true," said Cesar, leaning back in his chair and glancing out the window with a pensive look tinged with sorrow. "And just imagine the survival guilt that Fernando Parrado may have to bear, having lost both his mother and sister in the same accident. Yet I'm inclined to think that he'll weather it all. He's already shown an enormous capacity for psychological and physical survival."

"He certainly has," agreed Alice. "I've never heard of anyone with his kind of strength. And though it may sound kind of corny, I think it's really sort of inspiring."

"It sure is," said Panchi. "And who cares if it's corny. Which reminds me that I've cooked some corn for dinner, and it's time to eat."

"Sounds great," said Pepe. "But before we do, I'd like Cesar to tell Hank about his uncle, the one your mother was telling us about last weekend."

"Well, this is about my father's brother, who went down to the Tierra del Fuego region on some sort of expedition about sixty years ago. Anyway, they were caught in a blizzard and then a shipwreck which left them stranded on an ice-covered island, maybe a floe, where there were no food supplies of any kind—animal, vegetable, or mineral. Nothing at all. So, inevitably, they began to starve. Then, realizing there wouldn't be another ship in that desolate area for two or three weeks, they held a lottery to decide whose body would be sacrificed. And my uncle lost."

"My God! What a horrible—"

"But wait a minute. I haven't finished. . . . At any rate, they amputated his right leg, and it gave them enough nourishment to survive until a ship came by a week later."

"And your uncle lived?"

"That's right, Panchi. And, what's more, he himself survived by eating some of his own flesh."

"... But I'm Not a Hero"

On the following afternoon, December 29, thousands of Chileans went to the airport in Santiago to bid farewell to the survivors. Many went to emphasize their support, and to demonstrate their chagrin at the lurid headlines and news stories in the local press. But there were a few whose only reason for attending the going-away ceremony was nakedly morbid curiosity.

One middle-age matron frankly admitted her ulterior motive to the cab driver who drove her to the airport. "I want to see them face to face," she said, leaning forward to make sure he could hear. "I want to see how this cannibalism has changed their faces."

"How can you tell?" he asked, instantly regretting having given her an opening.

"Oh, you can always tell about something like that," she said, leaning closer. "You can see it in their eyes. The eyes are always a dead giveaway. The rest of the face can hide it—but never the eyes. And when you've done something as awful as eating your own friends, it has to show in your face—especially the eyes. . . ."

Temporarily wondering if he should kick her out at the next stoplight, yet not wanting to sacrifice a big fare to the airport, the driver simply clamped his mouth tight and refused to respond to anything else the woman said during the next forty minutes.

But neither she nor any other spectator had much of a chance for eye-to-eye contact with the Uruguayans, by this time weary of crowds. Surrounded by police and tight-lipped government officials, they were speedily hustled through the airport and into the waiting plane, which had been chartered by wealthy parents and relatives. Only ten survivors, however, were on board. Three of the original sixteen were already in Montevideo (Daniel Fernandez, Roberto Francois, and Alvaro Mangino); Roy Harley was still confined in a Santiago hospital; Fernando Parrado was vacationing in Vina del Mar; and Pedro Algorta was staying with relatives in Santiago.

Having been informed of the survivors' reluctance to go home by plane, the captain and his entire crew had informally discussed certain "antipanic strategies." The four stewardesses were especially attentive as the huge jet began its gradual ascent across the narrow San Fernando valley, climbing at a steeper angle as it veered eastward across the pre-cordillera toward the towering peaks just north of the majestic Tinguiririca. Some of the passengers forced themselves to look down at the dazzling maze of perpetually frozen mountains; others leaned away from the windows, holding tight to their arm rests with perspiring hands and silently mumbling a prayer.

"Try not to worry," said a dark-eyed stewardess in a soft, reassuring voice. "We'll be on the other side in just a few minutes."

"I'll try," was the answer. "Though it's not too easy to forget what it's like down there."

There was a general sigh of relief, a sheepish drying of moist palms on already damp handkerchiefs, as the plane approached the vast, mostly green pampa of Argentina. The group could relax now, perhaps visit with friends across the aisle, or simply close their eyes and speculate about the kind of questions they'd have to answer at the press conference in the familiar and perhaps more congenial ambience of El Colegio Stella Maris. Would the reporters be harsh and persistent? Would they probe for specific details? And what would be the attitude of the parents whose sons and daughters had not survived?

Curious, eager, skeptical, generally merciless but occasionally softhearted, the journalists themselves would have been unable to predict what their own reactions might be, for that would depend on the kind of answers they would get to questions they had all been eager to ask. Most of them were convinced the survivors had, indeed, eaten human flesh, and now they wanted to know what rationale had enabled them to overcome that most ancient taboo. Would there be direct answers? Or further evasions? Nearly one hundred correspondents were anxiously waiting to find out, some of them at the Montevideo airport, others at the school auditorium.

The sky was overcast, and there was a slight drizzle, which in no way discouraged the thousands of well-wishers who had started to gather two hours before the survivors' scheduled arrival. Upon express orders of President Juan Maria Bordaberry, whose two nephews were on the incoming flight, several hundred Air Force soldiers had established a tight cordon on both sides of the landing strip to keep reporters and photographers away from the plane. Relatives and friends, most of whom were jammed inside the waiting lounge, would also be restricted. The general public, which included hundreds of uniformed students from the Colegio Stella Maris, had been asked to wait on the second-floor terrace, where a carnival air of expectancy prevailed.

Shortly before 6:30 P.M., some of the students started yelling, "Here it comes," but they quickly quieted down when someone announced that it was only an Austral Airlines plane from Buenos Aires. Reporters later learned that among the passengers was the father of a young Uruguayan who had died in the crash. He was met in the tightly-packed reception area by his wife and three daughters, all of whom hugged him and wept silently as they pushed through a dense crowd at the door leading to the parking lot, with only a few bystanders aware of the poignant irony of his untimely arrival.

About a half hour later, the giant 707 burst through the leaden skies and zoomed onto the runway as a

huge roar rose up from the throats of thousands of
teary-eyed men, women, and children.

The plane made a complete turn in front of the airport tower and came to a stop about three hundred
feet from the main building. Two chartered buses,
which had been stationed near the luggage area all
afternoon, moved slowly toward the ramp as the first
passenger appeared at the doorway. It was Carlos
Paez, Jr., dressed in a bright blue sportshirt and gray
slacks, several good-luck charms dangling from his
neck and a large silver cross glistening in a television
spotlight as he waved at the tumultuous crowd. His
companions followed close behind, smiling and waving
as they came down the steps, each one shaking hands
with the President's wife, who was waiting at the bottom of the ramp with several government officials. But
there were two survivors who got more than a mere
handshake—her nephews, Eduardo and Adolfo Strauch
—whom she warmly embraced, tears welling in her
eyes. Then, surrounded by the welcoming committee
and their parents, who had accompanied them on the
flight, the survivors posed for group pictures while
waving to the yelling spectators on the terraces, after
which they quickly boarded the buses for the fifteen-
minute ride to the Colegio Stella Maris.

"We'll soon know what really happened," said an
Uruguayan reporter to Hans Topelmann, correspondent
for the German newspaper *Bild Zeitung,* as they got
into a cab to follow the buses.

"I already know what happened," replied Topelmann. "But I'm anxious to hear what rationale they'll
give."

"That's what I've been waiting for," said another
reporter. "And perhaps a few specific details on how
they managed to make those bodies more palatable."

As the cab pulled away, one of the newsmen glanced
at a handbill someone had been distributing inside the
airport, an advertisement of a soon-to-be-released
movie produced by a local film company: *Flight 502—
The Flight of Death.*

"My God," he said, crumpling the leaflet and tossing it out the window. "There's always some sick bastard exploiting a situation like this."

A short distance from the airport, the slow-moving procession of buses and cars turned left and proceeded down the Avenida Italia, where hundreds of people had been waiting under giant eucalyptus and bristly pines, while others waved greetings from the windows of stark-white mansions or slightly less opulent homes, most of which had red-tiled roofs, the familiar sights of suburban Carasco, where most of the survivors lived.

"This is where Parrado, Canessa, the Strauch brothers, and most of their teammates spent their childhood," said one of the Uruguayan reporters. "But that was a long time ago—they've suddenly become much older now."

"How so?" asked a Chilean colleague.

"This terrible accident, and all that came after, has robbed them of their youth," he answered. *"La Prensa* has just published the results of certain tests that were administered to these youngsters by Chilean specialists, and they showed astonishing changes. For example, one nineteen-year-old survivor was scored as having attained the maturity of a man forty-two years old. And he had raised his I.Q. by several points. The article also says that most of them will suffer severe psychological problems because of this premature drain on their brains."*

"Their conclusion may be right," someone commented. "But that reasoning is pure hogwash."

There was further conjecture among the press as the procession came closer to the school. Some newsmen had heard that one of the sixteen survivors had become *persona non grata* to his companions during their long ordeal—that he had complained too much, avoided his

---

* Author's note: It is difficult to believe anyone could have drawn such conclusions without reference to tests administered *before* the accident. Moreover, there is no evidence that such tests were given in Chile. But some Latin-American journals tend to specialize in this kind of wild speculation.

share of the routine chores, and occasionally filched extra rations.

"With the kind of *esprit de corps* I've seen among them, that's hard to believe," said a French reporter.

"Well, I don't find it at all difficult to believe," remarked an associate. "You've always got a sour apple in any barrel."

"Perhaps you're right. But there's one thing I admire in these kids: If they really had a bad apple among them, they've certainly kept it to themselves."

"They've kept an awful lot to themselves."

Having left their cab on a side street near El Colegio Stella Maris, the latecomer reporters rushed into the school gymnasium but found all the choice seats occupied. The television crews had set up their cameras and lighting equipment four hours earlier, their cables strewn across the floor like paralyzed eels. The improvised speakers' platform was surrounded by a squad of solemn-faced students with freshly pressed uniforms and red armbands. Another group was carefully checking the credentials of anyone attempting to get into the press section; a third squad was checking the identification of relatives and family friends; and a fourth platoon was guarding the honored guests' luggage and personal belongings. It was an impressive display of organizational skill and discipline.

"I'm beginning to see where Parrado and his friends got all the tough training that helped them survive," someone remarked. "They didn't come by it overnight."

But even highly disciplined student guards burst into wild cheers as the ten survivors walked into the gym after an unexplained delay of more than a half hour. When they finally did appear at exactly 8:00 P.M., one of the more cynical reporters commented that the television people were apparently controlling everything. Roberto Canessa was the first man in line, smiling and waving at the nearly hysterical crowd, reaching out to shake hands with friends. Behind him, also raising their hands in victory salutes, were Ramon Sabella, Gustavo

Zervino, Antonio Vicintin, Carlos Paez, Alfredo Delgado, Eduardo and Adolfo Strauch, Jose Luis Inciarte, and Javier Methol. Their lips still chapped, their eyes tinged with a weary sadness, they nevertheless kept smiling and raising their arms in response to a series of deafening hurrahs led by Daniel Juan, the middle-aged president of the Old Christian Club, whose members are alumni of the Colegio Stella Maris. Stepping away from the microphones as the crowd continued cheering, Juan finally quieted them with the palms-down hand signal.

When he had got complete silence, facing the spectators with a suddenly solemn expression, he leaned toward the mikes and softly said, "Now let's have a round of applause for those who died in that terrible tragedy."

Instantly responding, everyone rose as one person, yelling and clapping, stamping their feet, many of them embracing each other with tears running down their cheeks, others openly sobbing in spasms of uncontrollable grief. The ten survivors simply bowed their heads and wept silently. Probably expecting a less emotional response, Daniel Juan once again stepped away from the microphones and let the demonstration run its course.

Regaining the crowd's attention three or four minutes later, he announced the format of the two-part program: "Each one of our beloved boys will talk about a certain aspect of the long ordeal—after which they shall be happy to answer questions from the press. But no questions, please, until all of them have spoken."

Canessa was introduced first. His voice quiet but firm, with just the barest tremor of emotion, he described the immediate aftermath of the crash and spoke about the death of his best friend, Fernando Vasquez Nebel. "Seeing that he was badly injured, I asked him how he felt, and he said, 'I'm okay, Roberto, I can make it.' But he died a few minutes later." Explaining how some of the others had died almost instantly, he characterized their first night in the cordillera as one of the most horrifying he had ever experienced. "But the most sustained hardship was our final ten-day trip through and over that endless maze of snow-covered mountains. Fernando, as you undoubtedly know by now, carried me on his back after I had got hurt on the eighth day." Then recalling how nearsighted Parrado is, Canessa provoked gales of laughter when he told the crowd about Parrado's plan for killing one of the gentle old cows he had mistaken for a bull or at least a *wild* cow.

Vicintin was the next speaker, and he stressed how lucky he'd been in changing from one seat to another just before the plane crashed. Delgado talked about their deep despair when they heard the search had been abandoned, but emphasized their continued faith in God. Then Adolfo Strauch, Carlos Paez, and Ramon Sabella discussed the numerous methods they had devised to combat the cold at night and the glaring heat at midday. Eduardo Strauch came next, with a painfully remembered account of the avalanche, stressing the heroic rescue of several men who might have suffocated, then tearfully recalling the sudden deaths of eight other friends. He was followed by Zervino, who described various forays in search of the radio equipment inside the detached tail section, and in search of food and for a way out of the cordillera. Vicintin was then called back to talk about their weeklong preparation for the final go-for-broke expedition, wryly commenting on his having to leave the mission when Parrado realized they would need his rations.

Having already heard or read most of what they were saying, either in San Fernando or Santiago, some of the reporters became a shade impatient and fidgety, inwardly wondering if the survivors would finally get down to the big question—an outright admission of cannibalism or a continued refusal to talk about it.

But the next speaker, Jose Inciarte, seemed to be setting the stage for the long-awaited explanation of how they had managed to get enough food to stay alive. Inciarte still insisted on talking about the herbs and fungi he had supposedly discovered under the frozen snow, smiling when he mentioned the bees and flies he had seen. Strauch, on the other hand, detailed Roy Harley's rationing program: ". . . a tiny piece of chocolate, less than a teaspoon of coffee, paper-thin slivers of cheese, wine served in small caps of deodorant containers. . . ." (Incidentally, coffee had never been mentioned before.)

Having finally broached the much avoided subject of food, the survivors would now be expected to answer the ultimate question. Most of the press, sensing that the elders of the Old Christian Club were manipulating the scenario of the carefully structured presentation, had expected Roberto Canessa to deliver the group's answer, he being a medical student who could explain the intricacies of protein deficiency. But for reasons that would become more apparent later on, it was a third-year *law* student (Alfredo Delgado) who had been designated spokesman on that controversial issue.

With a keen sense of drama that will some day serve him well in a trial court, Delgado skillfully developed an appropriate emotional ambience, subtly shifting from one tense to another to pull his listeners into an extremely personal empathy:

". . . You wake up in the morning and gaze in wonder at the dazzling, snow-covered peaks all around you. And the silence of the cordillera is truly majestic —almost beyond belief. It's sometimes a frightening silence, which can make you feel terribly alone in a lost world—but I can assure you that God is always there. We all felt His presence, every one of us, even though we're not the kind of Catholics who chew our rosaries all day long and submerge ourselves in ritual. But when you are there, in the very midst of that awesome cordillera, you can feel the presence of God. Above all, you can feel what is sometimes called the Hand of God—which one interprets in many ways. As for us, there came the moment when all our supplies were exhausted, as well as the few things we could find when we had recovered enough strength to launch a few expeditions. And on the sixteenth day there comes a terrifying avalanche, which kills our dearest friends. They died, all of them, because, I believe—no, no, let me say *we* believe—God took them because they were the best of us, because each one of them, at the moment he died, gave us an example of courage and love.

"Whatever one tries to say about them, I think words can only serve to diminish the true dimension of what they meant to us. Each one of us carries them in our hearts, so there's no need to mention their valor, their specific deeds, their profound humanity, for words would merely lessen them. But, as I said before, there came that fatal moment when we had no more food— nothing, nothing at all to eat—and we thought to ourselves: If Christ at the Last Supper gave His body and His blood to His apostles, He was giving us to understand that we should do the same. So we, too, accepted the incarnation of His body and blood. And it meant to us a most intimate communion, the only thing that helped us stay alive. But we don't want this communion —which for us was an intimate, intimate, intimate act —to be desecrated or touched in any way. That is why we chose not to discuss it in a foreign land. But to you, our compatriots, we have come to say it as it should be said. Yet it should be taken and interpreted in its true dimensions."

There was total silence when Delgado finished his statement, a stunned silence, as if he had revealed a secret no one could possibly have imagined. Then, suddenly, someone started clapping, and within three seconds he was joined by everyone else in the gymnasium in prolonged thunderous applause. Gathering around Delgado, and along with him, the ten survivors embraced one another. And some of the parents, overcome with emotion, were assisted out of the room.

Daubing his eyes with the tip of his necktie, a middle-age Argentine reporter told a colleague that he had never heard such an eloquent statement. "Magnificent!" he said. "I wonder who helped him write it."

"A priest, probably," said one of his company. "That allusion to the Eucharist had a priestly touch."

"It must have been a cardinal," said an even more cynical European reporter. "No simple priest could have been that subtle. But he should have given St. Luke a little credit."

"But he wasn't referring to St. Luke, my friend. It's St. Matthew who quotes Jesus—'Take, eat; this is my body.' And then when he gave them the wine, he said, 'For this is my blood,' or words to that effect."

"Okay," said the cynic. "Then he should have given the credit to St. Matthew."

Obviously annoyed by their comments on Delgado's statement, an angry-faced Chilean correspondent snappishly interrupted them. "You're obviously assuming that Alfredo's speech was written for him—that his religious explanations were invented for him by a couple of priests. And I frankly resent your sarcasm."

"I'm sorry, *senor*. I was merely joking. It's one of my compulsions. But you'll have to admit that none of these boys had ever mentioned the Last Supper—not until tonight."

"Because they wanted to explain it here at home—among their own people."

The cynics, however, were far outnumbered by those who wholeheartedly accepted Delgado's mystical rationale. But many of them were frankly embarrassed by the maudlin excesses of Carlos Paez, Sr., who addressed the meeting a few minutes after the survivors had finished their dramatic accounts. With tears in his eyes and a preacherish tremor in his voice, the painter rambled from one metaphor to another, as if he were searching for the ultimate metaphor. Which he found:

". . . They suffered the Calvary of Christ—all sixteen becoming new Christs, young of age for those who don't believe in youth. And they didn't make as many stations as Christ did, because they had many more— I wish you could see the kind of stations there are in that snow, and the cold when it gets to your eyes and burns them. But what happens then? One day they come down from the mountains like the standard-bearers of Christ. And here they are. But they have dragged a different kind of cross—the cross of an airplane, an aluminum cross, and they've brought it to this world to prove that God exists, and that the faith must be maintained by people who, like them, really have open hearts, and who know that by struggling anything can be achieved. That's why I feel so uncomfortable at this microphone—because I'm taking the place that belongs to them. . . ."

Somehow mastering his modest discomfort, he stayed at the microphones a while longer, urging the survivors to become wandering apostles so as to spread the word of renewed faith. His speech was followed by a much less emotional talk by the father of Gustavo Zervino, who told the somewhat weary spectators about the parents' search efforts during the first few weeks following the crash.

Finally, the chairman announced they had reached the second part of the program, that the press would now be permitted to question the survivors on any facet of their tragic adventure. But not a single reporter accepted his offer. "We had all expected an avalanche of questions—some of them brutal," one reporter later recalled. "But everyone remained silent, some of us thinking Delgado had said all that could be said. Others, especially those with no religious faith, probably felt it would be unkind, insensitive, to ask for more specific details. And the word *canibalismo* was never spoken by anyone."

Later, several reporters interviewed the Auxiliary Bishop of Montevideo, Andres Rubio, for his reactions to the press conference. "I don't think there can be any criticism of what they did," he said quite emphatically. "Especially when one bears in mind that they acted out of extreme necessity. The Church respects the human body for what it has been. Because it has been, among other things, a temple of God, by virtue of baptism. But such bodies can be utilized to preserve life. It's my belief, therefore, that these sixteen youngsters have enlisted one of the forms of dignifying a deceased body. It's like the case of one who donates his eyes to a blind man, or any other transplant of a bodily organ."

When asked if one could therefore consider Turcatti's refusal to eat a form of suicide and therefore a violation of Catholic dogma, Bishop Rubio shook his head. "Of course not. You can say that those who ate the human flesh were in the right, and those who refused were also in the right. Any man who finds himself in an extreme situation has the right to resort to extreme measures to save his life. But he can't be *forced* to adopt such measures, and it would be wrong for anyone to try to force him against his will."

"Well, assuming that Turcatti did not commit suicide, could you say that eating human flesh was like taking communion?"

"Well, first of all, the refusal to eat was certainly not suicide; nor is it correct to characterize the consumption of human flesh as communion. One could say it was a kind of inspiration—but not communion."

There were others who shared the bishop's view. "It isn't necessary for these youngsters to seek exculpation in the Scriptures," remarked a local university professor the morning after the press conference. "They were perfectly justified on purely ethical grounds—certainly on scientific grounds. But perhaps Delgado's mystical reasoning will make their actions psychologically more acceptable, if indeed *they themselves* can genuinely accept the Eucharist rationale. Being neither Catholic nor Protestant, but simply a humble agnostic, I'm in no position to judge the psychic needs of these men, nor can I guess at what problems they'll face in the long run—when all this euphoria has faded away—especially when they come into direct face-to-face contact with the parents of those who didn't survive."

Fortunately, at least one such parent willingly expressed his views to the press, Dr. Helios Valeta, a distinguished gynecologist, whose son Carlos had fallen safely into the deep snow when the plane's tail section was ripped off, but who, while running toward his friends in the fuselage, happily waving his arms, had suddenly disappeared into a snow-covered crevice. Flanked by his wife and teen-age daughters, the gentle, soft-spoken doctor showed no trace of resentment.

"Like all the other parents," he said, "I was always hopeful. But somehow, from the very outset, I felt a horrible certainty that my son had already died. And when I heard on the radio that some of them were still alive, I immediately asked myself—since I am a doctor —'How could they possibly have survived?' Well, the simplest reasoning led me to the inevitable conclusion that they'd consumed the flesh of those who had died. There was no other way. And this, of course, posed several other rather horrifying questions: Who had made that decision? How was it done? And finally I had to wonder if my son—the body of my son—had been used to nourish the survivors. Now I know that it probably was. And I've accepted it, both as a doctor and as a father. I'm somehow comforted by the fact that those who died helped save the lives of sixteen others. Thus, in spite of my sorrow, I feel that my son's body had a more beautiful destiny than mere decomposition. And I prefer it that way. Every day thousands of people are saved by blood transfusions. And what, after all, is blood? It's just another human tissue— liquid, of course, but a tissue just the same. Yet no one is horrified by transfusions. Well, then, what happened in the cordillera is exactly the same. And that's why I accept it. But, you know, whenever a young mother whose baby I've just delivered asks me what she should name him, I'm tempted to tell her, 'Please call him Carlos, the name of my son.' "

For various personal reasons, six of the survivors were not present at the press conference; but the one whose absence was most apparent was Fernando Parrado, easily the most newsworthy member of the group. Consequently, conjecture was considerable as to his decision to remain at the Chilean resort, Vina del

Mar. Had he declined to join the others because of some antagonism toward Delgado's mystical rationale? Was he weary of the circus-like atmosphere which had surrounded them since December 22? Or, as some reporters surmised, was he a natural loner, who had no use for multiple drama? Whatever his reasons, Parrado attracted considerable attention when he returned on the morning after the meeting at Colegio Stella Maris. Arriving at Montevideo airport, waving at admirers who instantly recognized him as he descended the ramp, he hurried through customs accompanied by friends and relatives and shortly thereafter hopped into a white sports car that zoomed out of the airport at fifty or sixty miles an hour. Less than twenty minutes later he was home, surrounded by old friends who had been awaiting him in his father's elegant two-storey house in Punta Gorda, a lovely seaside suburb next to Carasco.

Rushing up to his room, perhaps to look at the familiar seascape from his terrace, Fernando must have smiled when he saw the walls plastered with numerous Walt Disney figurines—Pluto, Mickey Mouse, Donald Duck, and the Seven Dwarfs—which had replaced his favorite psychedelic posters. Only his blown-up photographs of Jim Clark, the auto-racing champion, were still in evidence. "They thought I was dead," he later explained to a reporter. "My father had been left alone, so he asked my sister and brother-in-law to come live with him, and my young nephews had taken over my room."

His father had also sold Nando's beautiful white motorcycle, a Suzuki 500, to his friend Pocholo, who had promptly returned it when the "Miracle of the Andes" was reported alive. Anxious to ride again, Parrado soon asked to be excused and rushed out to the garage, pausing temporarily to playfully wrestle with his dog, Jim. Then, his helmet strapped under his chin, he gunned the motor, crouched over the wide handlebars and skidded out of the driveway, eventually racing down the coast highway at 100 miles per hour.

Three days later, on the afternoon of January 2, Roy Harley Sanchez came home. The last of the sixteen survivors to return, he was greeted at the airport by a large crowd of admirers, who waved frantically and shouted *"Bienvenida! Bienvenida!"* from the visitors' terrace outside the second-floor dining room. None of them had been permitted to meet him in the landing area; nor were any reporters admitted into the roped-off section just off the runway, where his father's Mercedes-Benz had been parked. Only his parents, his brothers, and three friends—Paez, Inciarte, and Adolfo Strauch—were allowed to approach Roy as an airline attendant helped him down the stairs. Pale, emaciated, and barely able to walk, he paused for a moment and smiled weakly at the cheering crowd; then Paez and Inciarte aided him into the back seat of the car. Bypassing the customary exit from the airport, his father drove through the hangars of the adjacent Air Force Base, but, even so, several alert reporters were waiting at that exit.

"How do you feel?" one of them shouted through a half-opened window, having previously heard that Harley was still suffering from acute malnutrition.

"I'm all right," he said. "What more can I tell you? I guess it's a miracle that I'm still alive."

Turning to those around him, a teary-eyed teen-ager shouted, "Here comes the hero!"

"No, no—I'm not a hero," protested Harley. "Please don't say that. I'm not a hero."